A LARGER CHRISTIAN LIFE

A Larger Christian Life

A.B. SIMPSON

CHRISTIAN PUBLICATIONS

CAMP HILL, PENNSYLVANIA

Christian Publications
3825 Hartzdale Drive, Camp Hill, PA 17011

The mark of ✝ vibrant faith

ISBN: 0-87509-408-2
LOC Catalog Card Number: 88-70506
© 1988 by Christian Publications
All rights reserved
Printed in the United States of America

96 97 98 99 00   5 4 3 2 1

CONTENTS

INTRODUCTION

THE REISSUE OF ALBERT B. SIMPSON'S 1890 book, *A Larger Christian Life*, is timely. The Christian and Missionary Alliance, which Simpson founded, has entered its second century of world ministry and is pursuing faith-stretching goals for expansion and outreach. This book will help Alliance people gain their objectives.

When Simpson preached these sermons in 1890, *his* eye was focused on expansion and outreach. Alliance people were not fulfilling the task for which they had organized. How could they realize their goals? By a deepening and an enlargement of their Christian lives. That is what these messages were all about.

The first sermon—chapter one—was preached on the closing Sunday morning of the Old Orchard Convention, near Portland, Maine, July 29, 1890. Simpson coupled faith with prayer and challenged his listeners to sign a prayer pledge card—the *first* pledge card ever offered to Alliance people. He appointed a secretary for what he called the Prayer Alliance to tabulate the responses. Thousands signed.

Why the call for a Prayer Alliance? Because the Missionary Alliance, in three years (1887–1890), was scarcely realizing its purpose. Contributions were meager, missionary candidates were few. The situation had to be turned around, and Simpson intended his sermon to do just that.

When Simpson returned to his New York City Gospel Tabernacle, he preached on successive Sunday mornings (August 3 through September 28), nine of the other sermons you will read in this book. They were published, week by week, in his magazine. He preached the final sermon the closing Sunday of the Annual October Convention at the Tabernacle.

The sermons portray the level of Christian life necessary for the ministry the Lord expects from His church. You will find the terms "the sanctified life," "the Christ life," "the Spirit-filled life" and "the larger Christian life." The phrases differ, but each describes the same abundant, practical Christian experience at the heart of Simpson's preaching.

And what were the results? By the next year (1891), the floodgates of consecration and contributions had opened wide. At the end of the year, the Missionary Alliance had appointed 100 missionaries and had received the funds for their transportation and support. By 1897, more than 350 missionaries had sailed for foreign shores, and Alliance churches were multiplying throughout North America.

D.L. Moody is reported to have commented about Simpson's preaching: "No man gets to my heart like A.B. Simpson." Let these messages, now carefully updated for today's readers, get to *your* heart. May God use them to motivate you and, through you, His church.

John S. Sawin
Fort Myers, Florida
April 1988

The Possibilities of Faith

"Everything is possible for him who believes" (Mark 9:23).

THESE ARE BOLD and stupendous words. They open the treasure house of the Eternal King to man who was born in sin. To these children of clay, Jesus Christ offers the privilege of God's own omnipotence and all the possibilities of His infinite resources! Side by side with this promise stands another declaration that is just as astounding: "All things are possible with God" (Mark 10:27).

Salvation first

What are the possibilities of faith? Foremost is salvation. It does not matter how vile the sin or how multiplied or aggravated the guilt. Nor does it matter how deep the corruption or how long was the career of impenitence. "Whoever believes in the Son has eternal life" (John 3:36). "Believe in the Lord Jesus, and you will be saved" (Acts 16:31).

Sanctification is a second possibility to the person who believes. It is the Lord's will that we "receive . . . a place among those who are sanctified by faith in [Christ]" (Acts 26:18). Sanctification is not a work but a gift of grace, and all grace must be by faith. It is not possible by painful struggling, penance or self-torture. It is not possible by moral persuasion, careful training, correct teaching or perfect example. Sanctification is not made possible even by the dark, cold waters of death itself.

How *is* sanctification possible? Only by faith. It is the gift of Jesus Christ, the incoming and indwelling of Him. It is the interior life and divine imparting to us of the Holy Spirit, and it must be by faith alone. All this is possible to anyone who will believe, no matter how unholy he has been. He may be as mean and crooked as Jacob, as gross as David in his darkest sin, as self-confident as Simon Peter or as willful and self-righteous as Paul. Yet he can be and shall be made as spotless as the Son of God.

The possibility of divine healing

Still another possibility of faith for the one who believes is divine healing. "And the prayer offered in faith will make the sick person well; the Lord will raise him up" (James 5:15). The man or woman of faith still has access to this truth, a truth as true today as when the Master touched the eyes of the blind man to whom He said, "According to your faith it will be done to you" (Matthew 9:29).

It does not matter how serious the disease is. A person may be as helpless as the cripple whose friends lowered him through the roof to Jesus. Or his sickness may be as chronic as that which claimed the impotent man who lay helpless at the pool for 38 years. The malady may be as obscure and as despised as that of the poor blind man who begged by the wayside, whom the multitude thought unworthy of

Christ's attention. Or perhaps the sick one is as sinful as the Syro-Phoenician woman. Yet to her, as to others, healing came when Jesus could say "You have great faith! Your request is granted" (Matthew 15:28).

It is not the faith that heals; it is the God whom the faith touches. There is no other way of touching God except by faith. If we would receive His almighty touch, we must believe!

All power for service is a possibility to the man or woman of faith. The gift of the Holy Spirit is received by faith. The power of the apostles was in proportion to their faith. "Stephen, a man full of faith and of the Holy Spirit" (Acts 6:9) could meet all the wisdom of Saul of Tarsus and those in the synagogue of the Cilicians. The simple story of Barnabas is that "he was a good man, full of the Holy Spirit and faith, and a great number of people were brought to the Lord" (Acts 11:24).

The secret of effective preaching is not logic, rhetoric or eloquence, but to be able to say, "I believed; therefore I have spoken" (2 Corinthians 4:13). The success of some evangelists and Christian workers is out of all proportion to their talent or capacity in any direction, but they have one gift of expectancy that they faithfully exercise. They expect God to give them converts, and they are not disappointed.

The examples of a Moody or a Dr. Paul W. Harrison (American medical doctor to the Middle East who went out in 1894) are but types of what is possible for the humblest worker to accomplish if he but believes. If he wants powerful results, he must have his eye set only on the glory of God. He must possess a simple fidelity to the gospel of Christ. Then he will dare to expect the mightiest results.

Faith's omnipotence

All difficulties and dangers must give way before the omnipotence of faith. By faith the walls of Jericho fell down. Even today, the mightiest citadels of the adversary must give way before the steadfast and victorious march of faith. By faith Daniel stopped the mouths of lions and was delivered. It was not his uprightness of life or courageous fidelity that saved him—it was his confidence in Jehovah!

Such faith has carried intrepid missionaries through the jungles of Africa and South America. It has held back the stroke of death or some threatened disaster from many of us in the humbler experiences of our providential lives. The God of faith is still as near, as mighty and as true as when He walked with the Hebrew children through the fiery furnace or guarded the heroic Paul through all the perils of his changeful life. There is no difficulty too small for its exercise, no crisis too terrible for its triumph. Shall we go forth with this shield and buckler and prove the possibilities of faith? Then indeed shall we lead a charmed life despite the actions of our enemy and know that we are immortal until our work is done.

All the victories of prayer are possible to the person who believes. "If you believe, you will receive whatever you ask for in prayer" (Matthew 21:22). "I tell you, whatever you ask for in prayer, believe that you have received it, and it will be yours" (Mark 11:24). It is not the strength or length of the prayer that prevails, but the simplicity of its confidence.

It is the prayer of faith that claims the healing power of the unchanging Savior. It is the prayer of faith that reaches the soul that perhaps no human hand can approach, sometimes bringing from heaven the answer even before the echo of the petition has died away. In Cleveland, Ohio, a brokenhearted wife prayed earnestly with an evangelist for the soul of her lost husband. At that hour, the husband was led into a noontime Chicago prayer meeting. While the two in Cleveland prayed with faith, others in Chicago dealt with the man, and he was gloriously saved. The next day he sent the good news to his happy wife.

The prayer of faith raised enduring monuments on Ashley Down where 2,000 orphan children were fed daily by the hand of God in answer to the humble, believing cry of George Mueller. These are but patterns of what God, although hindered often by His people's unbelief, has always been ready to do.

These possibilities are open to each of us. We may not be called to public service or qualified for instructive speech or endowed with wealth and influence. But we are all given the power to touch the hand of omnipotence and minister at the altar of prevailing prayer. One censer we must bring—the golden bowl of faith. As we fill it with the burning coals of the Holy Spirit's fire and the incense of the great High Priest, there will be silence in heaven as God hushes the universe to listen. Then the living fire will be poured out upon the earth in the mighty forces of His providence and grace.

All joy and peace

All peace and joy are possible to the person of faith. The apostle's prayer for the Romans was that the God of hope would fill them with all joy and peace in believing (Romans 15:13). It is God's will and purpose that the unbelieving soul shall be an unhappy soul and that those whose minds are stayed upon God and trusting in Him shall have perfect peace. Would you like to be happy even in the darkest hour? Then trust in the Lord and dwell continually in Him (Isaiah 26:3). Would you like to know the peace that is beyond understanding? Then be anxious about nothing and steadfastly believe that the Lord is at hand, supreme above every circumstance and causing all things to work together for good to those who love Him (Philippians 4:6-7; Romans 8:28).

Would you like the perennial overflowings of joy? Then learn the truth of First Peter 1:8 – "Though you have not seen him, you love him; and even though you do not see him now, you believe in him and are filled with an inexpressible and glorious joy." The joy of mere paroxysmal laughter and motion is like the cut flower on a brief winter's day. It is separated from the root and withers before another sunset. The joy of faith is the fruit and perpetual bloom that covers the living tree or the rooted plant in a watered garden.

The evangelization of the world is yet another possibility of faith. The most successful missionary operations are sustained wholly through faith in God and the power of prayer. There is no field of faith as vast and sublime as the mission field today, and the possibilities which faith may claim are unlimited. What great opportunity this presents to those of us who would be workers together with God for the greatest achievement of all the Christian centuries!

The Lord's coming will doubtless be founded at last on faith. There will be a generation who will say, "Surely this is our God; we trusted in him, and he saved us" (Isaiah 25:9). As yet it is our blessed hope, but it will some day be ours in its fullness. Reading both earth and sky—the tokens of His coming—His waiting Bride will hear the glad cry, "The wedding of the Lamb has come" (Revelation 19:7). To Simeon of old it was made known that he should see the Lord's Christ. In like manner, to the righteous in the last times the Morning Star shall rise. May the Lord help us to so understand our times and the work our Master expects of us in preparation for His coming that we shall share in the recompense of faith and even hasten that joyful day.

All things

Beyond all that has been said, this scriptural promise means that *all* things are possible to the person who will believe God. It is possible to have any or even many of the achievements listed here and still miss the *all* things of God's highest will. The full meaning of this promise is that faith may claim a complete life, where nothing shall be lacking, a finished service and a crown lacking no jewel of recompense. Some lives are not wholly lost, but they are not saved to the uttermost. Many of us are coming short of all that God has had in His highest thought for us.

When the king of Israel stood by the bedside of the dying prophet of the Lord, Elisha put his hand upon the hands of Joash and helped him shoot the arrows that were symbolic of faith and victory. Then the prophet required that the king should follow up this act of mutual faith by a more individual expression of expectation. Sadly, as it is with most of us, his faith evaporated long before its needed work was done. He struck the ground only three times and stopped. It was too late for him to recover his lost blessing. The grieved and actually angry prophet upbraided him for his smallness of heart. He told him sorrowfully that his blessing would be limited according to the measure of his faith (2 Kings 13).

Never will I forget the solemnity with which God brought this passage to my soul. It was in a crisis of my life, and this text seemed to ask how much I would take from God and how little would satisfy my faith. Thank God, He enabled me to say with a bursting heart, "I want nothing less than all of Your highest will, all of faith's greatest possibilities!" May the Lord help us to live each day under the power of those holy aspirations and see their true value. This will bring us to cherish the same lofty ambition with Paul, "I consider my life worth nothing to me, if only I may finish the race and complete the task the Lord Jesus has given me—the task of testifying to the gospel of God's grace" (Acts 20:24).

Christian, are you missing anything from your life, your one, precious, narrow span of earthly opportunity, the pivot on which eternity revolves—the one eternal possibility that will never return again? God is waiting to give you all, and all things are possible to everyone who believes.

Everything depends on faith

Because the ruin of the race began with the loss of faith, its recovery must come through the exercise of faith. The poison Satan injected into the blood of Eve was the strychnine of unbelief. She questioned God's faithfulness. The one prescription the gospel gives to the lost is this: "Believe on the Lord Jesus, and you will be saved" (Acts 16:31).

Faith is the law of Christianity, the vital principle of the gospel dispensation. Paul calls it the law of faith, in distinction from the law of works. The Lord Jesus expressed it in the simple formula that has become the standard of answered prayer and of every blessing we receive through the name of Jesus. God is therefore bound to act according to our faith *and* our unbelief!

Faith is the only way known to us by which we can accept a gift from God. All the blessings of the gospel are the gifts of grace; therefore, they must come to us through faith. Furthermore, they will come only in the measure of our faith.

Faith is necessary to strengthen and prepare our own hearts for the reception of God and His grace. Without it, how can the Father communicate His love to a timid, trembling heart? How can God come near to a frightened child? A tiny bird may actually die of terror in the hand of one whose only intent is to caress it and win its love. Even so, the heart without faith would faint from terror in the presence of God, unable to receive the overflowing love of the Father whom it could not understand.

Faith is an actual spiritual force. It is no doubt one of the attributes of God Himself. We find it exemplified in Jesus in all His miracles. He explains to His disciples that it was the power by which He withered the fig tree. And it was the power by which they could overcome and dissolve the mightiest obstacles in their way. There is no doubt that while the soul is exercising, through the power of God, the faith that commands what God commands, a mighty force is operating at that moment upon the obstacle. God has put into our hands one of His own implements of omnipotence and permitted us to use it in the name of Jesus, according to His will and for the establishment of His kingdom.

The preeminent reason why God requires faith is that faith is the only way through which God Himself can have absolute room to work. This is true because faith is that colorless, simple attitude by which man ceases from his own works and enters into the work of God. It is the difference between the human and the divine, the natural and the supernatural. The reason faith is so mighty and indeed, omnipotent, is that it makes way for the omnipotence of God.

The two sentences are strangely and exactly parallel: "All things are possible with God" and "Everything is possible for him who believes." The same power is possessed by both God and the person who believes. This is so because the latter is lost in, and wholly identified with, the former. Surrendering our own insufficiency, we link up with the all-sufficiency of God and go forth triumphantly exclaiming: "I can do everything through him who gives me strength" (Philippians 4:13), and heaven echoes back, "Everything is possible for him who believes!"

The hindrances to faith

Of course, we need scarcely say that faith is dependent upon obedience and rightness of heart and life. We cannot trust God in the face of willful sin. Even an unsanctified state is fatal to any high degree of faith, for the carnal heart is not the soil in which it can grow. The fruit of the Spirit is always hindered when the heart is overgrown with the weeds of sin and willful indulgence. The reason a great many Christians have so little faith is because they are living in the world and in themselves and are living to some degree apart from God and His holiness.

When an observatory is about to be built, the site

selected is always on some high mountain. The aim is to find a place where there is a clear, unobstructed view of the heavens. Similarly, faith requires for its heavenly vision the highlands of holiness and separation, the pure sky of a consecrated life.

Faith is also hindered by the weak and unscriptural way that so many excuse their unbelief and lightly speak of the sin of doubting God. If we would have strong faith, we must recognize it as an imperative, sacred obligation. Then let us steadfastly and firmly believe God and refuse to ever doubt Him.

Let us never say we cannot believe. While in ourselves we are unable, God has provided us with that power to believe Him if we will only choose to do so. Let us no longer condone and palliate our doubts as harmless infirmities and sad misfortunes. Rather "see to it, brothers, that none of [us] has a sinful, unbelieving heart that turns away from the living God" (Hebrews 3:12).

Faith is further hindered by reliance upon human wisdom, whether our own or that of others. The devil's first bait to Eve was an offer of wisdom, and for this she sold her faith! "You will be like God," he said, "knowing good and evil" (Genesis 3:5), and from the hour she began to "know" she ceased to trust.

The spies were the ones who lost the land of promise to Israel. It was their foolish proposition to search out the land and find out whether God had told the truth that led to the awful outbreak of unbelief, thereby shutting the doors of Canaan to a complete generation. It is significant that the names of nearly all these spies are suggestive of human wisdom, greatness and fame.

So it was, too, in the days of Christ. The traditions

of the elders and the opinions of men kept them back from receiving Him. "How can you believe if you accept praise from one another, yet make no effort to obtain the praise that comes from the only God?" (John 5:44). This, today, has much to do with the limitations of the church's faith. The Bible is measured by human criticism, and the promises of God are weighed in the balances of natural probability and human reason.

Our own wisdom is just as dangerous if it takes the place of God's simple word. Therefore if we are determined to trust the Lord with all our heart, we must not lean on our own understanding (Proverbs 3:5).

Hindered by our own strength

Another hindrance to faith is self-sufficiency and dependence on our own strength. Before we can be brought to trust in God, He has to reduce us to helplessness. The hour of His mightiest interposition is usually the time of our greatest extremity.

Has God brought you to the end of your strength? Rejoice and be exceeding glad, for it is the beginning of His Omnipotence! If faith will but fall into His mighty arms and cry out like those of old, "Lord, there is no one like you to help the powerless against the mighty. Help us, O Lord our God, for we rely on you, and in your name we have come against this vast army" (2 Chronicles 14:11).

Faith is hindered by sight and sense and our foolish dependence upon external evidences. The very evidence in which we must live and grow is the unseen. All outward things, therefore, must be withdrawn before we can truly believe. Then, as we look not at the things that are seen but on the things which are not seen, they grow real—more real than the things of sense. God then makes them real in actual accomplishment. But first, faith must step out into the great unknown and walk on the water to go to Jesus—no, it is more like walking on nothing but air. In the center of emptiness, faith will still find a rock beneath its feet!

There is a story of a traveler in the Alps who had reached the end of a long mountain path. The path had suddenly disappeared beneath a great mass of ice and snow and a subterranean torrent. There stood the towering mountain sternly blocking his way ahead. Miles of desolation lay behind him. What should he do? With only a word of instruction, his guide exclaimed, "Follow me!" Then he plunged into the churning water and disappeared from sight. It was a dreadful thing, but he must follow or die! There was the sudden shock of the icy water, the whirl of that plunging current, an awful darkness and then a sudden, beautiful burst of light! Catching his breath, he found himself lying on the sunny banks of a quiet stream. He had made it to the other side of the mountain through the very channel dug by that mighty flow of water! The unseen way had led to life and light.

Even so, faith still walks frequently in paths of mystery, but God will always make it plain. Is it not a hindrance to our faith when we hesitate to believe God before we venture upon the naked word of His promise? Your faith alone is the substance of things hoped for, the evidence of things not seen (Hebrews 11:1). God help us to walk by faith and not by sight!

Because these things are true, God has to train us in the way of faith by difficulties, trials and seeming refusals, until, like the Syro-Phoenician woman, we simply trust on and refuse to be refused. He is always waiting to recompense our trust by the glad words, "You have great faith! Your request is granted" (Matthew 15:28).

Hindered by our own faith

Finally, faith is hindered most of all by what we call "our faith." In a fruitless effort, we struggle to work out a faith that, after all, is but a make-believe, desperate trying to trust God. But this will always come short of His vast and glorious promise. The truth is that the only faith that is equal to the stupendous promises of God and the measureless needs of our life is "faith in the Son of God" (Galatians 2:20). The faith we need is that which God will breathe into the heart that intelligently, expectantly looks to Him. His faith will give us the power to live, obey and perform any other exercise of the new life.

Blessed be His name! He has not given us a chain that is one link short of aiding our poor, helpless heart. His chain of love is just as divine where it binds the human side as where it links us up to His throne of promise in the heavens. "Have faith in God" (Mark 11:22). "I live by the faith of the Son of God." That was the victorious testimony of one who had proved it true.

In the light of this great provision, listen to the mighty promise now, and in His faith rise up to claim it. "Everything is possible for him who believes." Then cry out to Him, "I do believe. Help me overcome my unbelief!" (Mark 9:24).

This mighty engine of spiritual power is placed in our hands by Omnipotent Love. Shall we claim it and, by the help of God, rise to its utmost possibilities? From this hour, shall we turn this heavenly weapon upon the field of Christian life and conflict? Let us use it for all that God has called us to in the great conflicts of the age and for the kingdom of our Lord and Savior, Jesus Christ.

2

The Joy of the Lord

The joy of the Lord is your strength (Nehemiah 8:10).

THERE IS NO MORE POINTED difference between Christianity and all other religions than the element of joyfulness. The natural countenance of heathenism is gloomy and often profoundly sad. But the true expression of a consecrated face is radiance and gladness. True, this is not always realized as it ought to be. When the Holy Spirit shines in the sanctified heart, though, the face reflects its glory and, like Stephen's, is often like the face of an angel. Writing his account of one of our conventions, a newspaper reporter stated: "One thing that characterized all the faces was their wonderful joyfulness." Surely this ought always to be true.

Why? Because "God is light. In him there is no darkness at all" (1 John 1:5). The blessed God must be the source of blessedness. His beloved Son, our Pattern and our Savior, is the Prince of Peace and the Royal Bridegroom whom God "anointed with the oil of joy" (Hebrews 1:9). His salvation should be a glad salvation. His touch should bring joy and sunshine. Those who follow Him should fellowship in that happy company who "will enter Zion with singing;

everlasting joy will crown their heads. Gladness and joy will overtake them, and sorrow and sighing will flee away" (Isaiah 35:10).

As we look over the earth, we find that God has put beauty and gladness wherever He can. He wants us to be happy, and He has sent redemption to restore and consummate our joy. His great salvation, therefore, is inseparably linked with a rejoicing spirit. It cannot stoop to sorrow and will not dwell in gloom. It must banish sorrow as well as sin and live in the light of joy.

We must, then, give up trying to combine religion and melancholy, for Christ will have none but a happy people. Even old Judaism robed itself in bridal garments whenever it could and went forth with songs of rejoicing. Under the Mosaic Law, there was a constant succession of feasts. In the closing festival of the sacred year, the Israelites were required to spend an entire week in the most romantic and picturesque religious rejoicing. They dwelt in rustic booths and united in festal services with sacred songs and ceremonies that must have formed a grand and impressive spectacle of national rejoicing.

In our Scripture, it was the Feast of Tabernacles that Nehemiah and the people were observing. Yet, like some of us, they had come with long faces. They thought it becoming for them to celebrate the occasion with a few appropriate tears. After all, they were thinking of the desolations of Zion that had just been removed and restored. But Nehemiah told them that just because it was a holy day did not mean it was time for mourning. Holiness and tears did not go well together. The sorrows were past. There was no longer any cause for mourning. This was to be a day of gladness and praise, and the spirit of praise was necessary in order to even prepare for their present tasks. So he proclaimed: "the joy of the Lord is your strength."

The Source of strength

Look at the ordinary duties of daily life. Consider how much you can do when your heart is light and free. On the other hand, remember how long and heavy the easiest task is when it is irksome. A father can sweat all day at his work for the joy of knowing that his efforts are for his family. A laborer can brighten his work with a little song, keeping rhythm with his actions. A soldier can shorten his long days by a bit of music or the beat of a drum.

John Bunyan puts it happily when he tells us how he wrote the *Pilgrim's Progress* in his old Bedford dungeon: "I sat me down and wrote and wrote, because joy did make me write." The old dungeon with its stinted rays of light, its clumsy table and stool and its pallet of straw for a bed was like heaven to him, because the joy of Pilgrim's home and story was bursting in his happy heart.

We need this kind of joy in the plodding drudgery of our daily routine in the factory, the shop, the store, the kitchen, the office—in the dullness of isolation or the monotony of publicity. Circumstances will make little difference where the everlasting springs are bursting from the deep well of God's joy in our hearts!

> The joy of the Lord is our strength for life's
>   burden,
>   And gives to each duty a heavenly zest;
>   It sets to sweet music the task of the toiler,
>   And softens the couch of the laborer's rest.

David has expressed this blending of common life with heavenly gladness in Psalm 119: "Your decrees are the theme of my song wherever I lodge" (verse 54). David found delight in setting to music the statutes of the Lord, and thus translated to ceaseless praise God's call to daily duty. This is the meaning of the entire psalm. It is all about duty, and yet it is the most exquisitely constructed portion of the Hebrew Psalter. As someone has said, it is duty set to music. This is the way to make duty easy and acceptable to God.

Let us take the joy of the Lord into the dark places, the hard and low places, into the dusty and grimy streets of life. Let us learn to rejoice in the light and to go through this common life so filled with the Spirit that, like men intoxicated with the wine of heaven, we will "speak to one another with psalms, hymns and spiritual songs" (Ephesians 5:19). Then it will be true that "Whatever you do, whether in word or deed [you will] do it all in the name of the Lord Jesus, giving thanks to God the Father through him" (Colossians 3:17).

Strength for trials

The joy of the Lord is our strength for the trials of life. There are two ways of bearing a trial. The one is with the spirit of stoic endurance, and the other is through the counteracting forces of a holy and victorious joy. It was through this latter way that Christ endured the cross — "for the joy set before him" (Hebrews 12:2).

In the first chapter of Colossians, we read the prayer of the apostle for a certain company of saints. These individuals had already reached such a measure of holiness that they were made partakers of the inheritance of the saints in light. But there was something higher and better for them. Namely, that they should be "strengthened with all power according to his glorious might so that [they] might have great endurance and patience, and joyfully [give] thanks to the Father" (Colossians 1:11).

The patience would be to endure the trials from the hand of God, and the longsuffering or endurance was to endure the trials that come from men. In either case, the endurance was to be experienced with real joyfulness. And so the apostle explains his self-sacrifices for the Philippians: "Even if I am being poured out like a drink offering on the sacrifice and service coming from your faith, I am glad and rejoice with all of you" (Philippians 2:17).

The Hebrew Christians were congratulated because they had sympathized "with those in prison and joyfully accepted the confiscation of [their] property, because [they] knew that [they themselves] had better and lasting possessions" (Hebrews 10:34). This is not a common experience. Some women lose their sanctification over a dish broken by a careless helper or a new tablecloth or dress spotted by spilled coffee. Some men get angry when the mistakes or failures of employees injure their business or cause them to lose large sums of money.

The joy of the Lord always counts on something better than that which we lose and remembers that there is One above who is the great Recompenser and Restorer. In the future, He will give a thousand times more honor for one victory of patience and love than all the world is worth today.

> Yes, the joy of the Lord is our strength for life's
> trials,
>> And lifts up the heart crushed by sorrow and
>> care,
> Like the nightingale's song, it can sing in the
> darkness,
>> And rejoice when the fig tree is withered and
>> bare.

Strength over temptation

The joy of the Lord is our strength over temptation.
"Consider it pure joy, my brothers," James says,
"whenever you face trials of many kinds" (1:2). This is
the best way to meet trials. The devil always gets the
best of a melancholy soul. Despondency will always
bring surrender. Joy in his own home is so foreign to
Satan that a happy face always scares him away. Ama-
lek got hold of the hindmost part of Israel's camp —
the discouraged ones who were dragging behind and
fretting about the hot weather and the hard road they
had to travel. The fiery serpents, which were the
devil's scouts, stung the murmuring multitudes, and it
was an upward look to the brazen serpent that healed
them. Jehoshaphat's armies marched to battle and victory with shouts of faith and songs of praise. And to
this day, the joy of the Lord is the best equipment for
the great conflict.

But the apostle also means, no doubt, that temptation is no cause for despondency. Rather, it is a great
opportunity for spiritual progress. It is the proving of
our armor and an evident token that the devil sees
something in us worth trying to steal. We may be sure
that where the army of the enemy is encamped, there
the army of the Lord is also near. "You know that the

testing of your faith develops perseverance. Perseverance must finish its work so that you may be mature and complete, not lacking anything" (James 1:3).

Let us go through all the discipline and learn all that it has to teach us, because "Blessed is the man who perseveres under trial, because when he has stood the test, he will receive the crown of life that God has promised to those who love him" (James 1:12). Let us go then, without fear of a cloud, into the conflicts that lie ahead. When we cannot feel the joy of having to "suffer grief in all kinds of trials" (1 Peter 1:6), then let us declare, "I delight greatly in the Lord; my soul rejoices in my God" (Isaiah 61:10).

> The joy of the Lord is our strength for
>   temptation,
>   And counts it the testing of patience and grace;
> It marches to battle with shouts of salvation,
>   And rides o'er its foes in the chariots of praise.

Our strength for the body

The joy of the Lord is our strength for the body. "A cheerful heart is good medicine" (Proverbs 17:22). This is the divine prescription for a weak body. On the other hand, despondency and depression of spirit are the causes of nervousness, headaches, heartbreak and low physical vitality. A word of cheer and an impulse of hope and gladness will often break the power of disease.

I remember a dying man whom I visited in the early years of my ministry. He was declared a hopeless case by his doctors and pronounced to be near death. As I visited him for what I supposed would be the last time and tenderly led him to the Savior, he accepted the gospel and became filled with the peace of God. The joy of salvation came upon him with a baptism of glory and inspiration, and the rapture of heaven was so evident, that he kept us for hours beside his bed as he shouted and sang what we all believed to be the first of the songs of heaven! We said goodnight long after midnight, fully expecting him to be gone to glory by morning. But so mighty was the uplift in his soul, that his body threw off the power of disease, and the next morning, to the doctors' amazement, he was improved. Within a few days, he was entirely well!

At that time, I knew nothing of divine healing. But I had witnessed, with astonishment and delight, the power of divine joy to heal disease. Many times since then I have seen the healing and the gladness of Jesus so come to the soul and body that the night of weeping turned into a morning of joy!

It is true that there is a deeper cause and a more divine power than the mere natural influence of joy. Incurable disease will yield only to the actual touch of divine omnipotence. But joy is the channel through which the healing waters flow. After that, there comes the overflow of the life of Christ in both the soul and body.

If you long to live above your physical condition; if you would renew your strength continually and "soar on wings like eagles," "run and not grow weary" and "walk and not grow faint" (Isaiah 40:31); if you would carry in your veins the exhilaration and zest of unwearied youth and freshness, then rejoice in the Lord at all times. If you want to experience in all its fullness a foretaste of the resurrection life in your body; if you would be armed against the devil's shafts of infirmity and pain and throw off those arrows like glowing iron repels water, then "Rejoice in the Lord always" (Philippians 4:4).

Strength for service

The joy of the Lord is our strength for service and testimony. It makes all our work easy and delightful. It gives a perpetual spring in the hardest fields of Christian service. It goes with the foreign missionary and the one who works all night in the heart of the slums. The joy of the Lord takes away the natural tendency to shrink back from the degraded and unclean, from the horror of filth and vermin, from the fear of violent and wicked men and from all the repulsiveness and hideousness of the surrounding scenes. As for the work that would be naturally revolting, heavenly joy makes it fascinating! It enables the consecrated heart to say, "None of these things move me, neither count I my life dear unto myself, so that I might finish my course with joy, and the ministry, which I have received of the Lord Jesus, to testify the gospel of the grace of God" (Acts 20:24).

Not only does it give a constraining motive to our service, but it also gives it a divine effectiveness and power. It illuminates the face with the light of heaven and melts the voice with accents of tenderness and love. It gives our words a weight and winning power that men cannot resist. They know that we possess a secret to which they are strangers, and our gladness awakens their longing to share our joy.

A scholarly minister once gave a course of lectures on the "Evidences of Christianity" for the special purpose of convincing and converting a wealthy and influential skeptic in his congregation. The man attended the lectures and was soundly converted. A few days later, the minister ventured to ask him which of the lectures had persuaded him to make his commitment to Christ. "The lectures?" he responded. "I don't even remember the subject of your lectures, and I cannot honestly say that they made any decisive influence on my mind. But I was converted when I heard the testimony of that dear old black woman who attended those services. As she hobbled up the steps near me, her glad face was as bright as heaven. Night after night she would say, 'My blessed Jesus! My blessed Jesus!' Then she would turn to me and ask, 'Do you love my blessed Jesus?' That, sir, was my evidence of Christianity."

Praise the Lord! We can all shine like that — *burning* as well as *shining* lights — and set hearts aglow with the contagion of our joy! The world is looking for happiness, and if it finds the secret in genuine form, it will try to get it. Charles Finney tells of attending prayer meeting, on occasion, before his conversion. There the deacons would ask him, "Would you like us to pray for you?"

"No," he replied. "I would be very sorry to have you pray for me. In the first place, if I were converted through your prayers, I would probably become as miserable as you are. And in the second place, I do not believe your prayers would have any power to bring about my conversion. In fact, I suspect that you would even be a good deal surprised if anything happened, for you have been praying in the same melancholy way, asking for revival, ever since I came to this town. Yet I can see by the tone of your voices and the look on your faces that you have no idea that it is ever coming. When I am converted, I want a religion that will make me happy and a God who will do what I ask of Him."

May the Lord save us from religious melancholia and send us out to work for Him with shining faces, victorious accents and hearts overflowing with contagious joy. Then, like Stephen, we will be able to look into the faces of our enemies and confound them by our countenances. That will force the world to take notice of us — notice that we have been with Jesus!

> Let the joy of the Lord be the strength of our
> service,
> To speak through our faces and accents of love,
> And show all this sad world the fullness of Jesus,
> So each hungry heart His salvation may prove.

The secret of this joy

The joy of the Lord springs from the assurance of salvation. It is the joy of salvation. Its happy song is,

> Blessed assurance, Jesus is mine,
> Oh, what a foretaste of glory divine!
> Heir of salvation, purchased of God,
> Born of His Spirit, washed in His blood.
> This is my story, this is my song,
> Praising my Savior all the day long.

If you would know this joy, you must accept God's promise with full assurance of faith and rest upon His word without wavering or doubting.

This joy is the joy of the Holy Spirit. "The fruit of the Spirit is . . . joy" (Galatians 5:22). It is not indigenous to earthly soil; it is a plant of heavenly birth. It belongs to the kingdom of God. To know this joy, we must receive the baptism of the Spirit in full surrender and simple faith. It is characteristic of all who receive this baptism that they know the joy of the Lord. Until we receive this eternal fountain in our heart, all our attempts at joy are but surface wells. They are waters often defiled, and their bottoms are often dry. We talk about the great Artesian stream, the "spring of water welling up to eternal life" (John 4:14).

This joy of which we speak is likewise the joy of faith. "May the God of hope fill you with all joy and peace as you trust in him" (Romans 15:13). There is indeed a deep delight when God has answered prayer and the joy of fulfillment and possession overflows with thankfulness. But there is a more thrilling joy when the heart first commits itself to God's naked promise. Standing on His simple word in the face of natural improbability or seeming impossibility, it declares, "Though the fig tree does not bud and there are no grapes on the vines, though the olive crop fails and the fields produce no food, though there are no sheep in the pen and no cattle in the stalls, yet I will rejoice in the Lord, I will be joyful in God my Savior" (Habbakuk 3:17).

If you are doubting God, you need not wonder that your joy is intermittent. The witness of the Spirit always follows the act of trust. "You will keep in perfect peace him whose mind is steadfast, because he trusts in you" (Isaiah 26:3). It is just as true conversely that "if you do not stand firm in your faith, you will not stand at all" (Isaiah 7:9).

Sustained by His Word

The joy of the Lord is sustained by His Word and nourished by His "very great and precious promises" (2 Peter 1:4). "I rejoice in your promise," exclaims the psalmist, "like one who finds great spoil" (Psalm 119:162). There is rich delight in beholding, in the light of the Holy Spirit, the heavenly landscape of truth open before the spiritual vision. It is like some land of promise shining in the glory of the sunlight, the whole Bible seeming like the vision Moses saw from the top of Mt. Pisgah! We have found great spoil, and it is all our own. "We have not received the spirit of the world but the Spirit who is from God, that we may understand what God has freely given us" (1 Corinthians 2:12). Therefore, we can truly say like the psalmist, "Your statutes are my delight; they are my counselors" (Psalm 119:24).

Do you know the joy that lies hidden in the Bible's neglected pages, the honey that you might drink from this garden of the Lord, these blossoms of truth and promise? Take the Bible as the living love letter from His heart to yours. Ask Him to speak it to you in joy and faith and spiritual illumination.

It is the joy of prayer, this joy of the Lord. Its element is the secluded prayer room, and its source is the mercy seat. No prayerless life can be a happy one. "Ask and you will receive, and your joy will be complete" (John 16:24).

> This is the place where Jesus sheds
>   The oil of gladness on our heads;
> The place than all besides more sweet,
>   It is the blood-bought Mercy-seat.

The joy of the Lord is the joy of meekness and love. "The humble will rejoice in the Holy One of Israel" (Isaiah 29:19), and the loving spirit always finds that "it is more blessed to give than to receive" (Acts 20:35). Selfishness is misery; love is life and joy. The gentle, lowly, chastened spirit will find all the flowers in bloom and the waters flowing in the valleys of humility.

Do you know the gladness that comes from yielding to the will of God, from bearing patiently the wrong or from being silent under the word of reproach? Have you learned the joy of returning good for evil, of offering that word of comfort to the sorrowing heart or the cup of cold water to a thirsty pilgrim? Have you experienced the loss of your own pleasure so that what you saved could be given to the Lord? Then it is that all the bells of joy are heard softly ringing and the Master whispers to your glad and trembling heart, "You did it for me" (Matthew 25:40).

Joy of service

This joy of the Lord is the joy of service — especially the winning of souls to Christ. All true work is a natural delight, but work for God in the true spirit and in the power of the Holy Spirit is the partnership of His joy. If you wish for a life lifted above a thousand temptations and petty cares, be busy for your Master, and let each moment see

> Some work of love begun
> Some deed of kindness done;
> Some wanderer sought and won,
>   Something for Thee.

We cannot convey the Living Water to another heart without being watered ourselves on the way. There is no joy more exquisite than the joy of leading a person to Christ. It is like the mother's strange, instinctive rapture over her newborn baby.

Do you know the ecstasy of feeling the new life

of an immortal spirit sweeping through your veins? How thrilling it is to kneel by the side of one freshly born into God's family—born to die no more! How wonderful it is to place that newborn infant into the arms of the Savior! It is the joy of angels, setting all the harps of heaven to ringing. And surely it would be strange if this were not the higher joy of ransomed saints.

The joy of the Lord is also the joy of a faithful servant. There is a sense even here in which, as often as we are true to God and faithful to the call of duty and opportunity, His Spirit gives us a present reward. It is a baptism of joy with a whisper to the faithful heart, "Well done, good and faithful servant! Come and share your master's happiness!" (Matthew 25:23).

The joy of hope

It is likewise the joy of hope. "We rejoice in the hope of the glory of God" (Romans 5:2). It is the reflected light of the coming Sunrise and the millennial day. Except for the death and resurrection of Jesus and the baptism of the Holy Spirit, there is nothing that brings us more divine gladness than the blessed hope of the Lord's coming. It is indeed "a light shining in a dark place" (2 Peter 1:19)—the Morning Star that presages the Rising Sun.

Then finally, the joy of the Lord is the joy of Christ Himself within us. "I have told you this so that my joy may be in you and that your joy may be complete" (John 15:11). This is the deepest secret of spiritual joy. It is the indwelling Christ Himself rejoicing in the heart as He rejoiced in the darkest hour of His life on earth. Now in heaven, He realizes the fulfillment of His own messianic words in Psalm 16: "Therefore my heart is glad and my tongue rejoices; my body also will rest secure, because you will not abandon me to the grave, nor will you let your Holy One see decay. You have made known to me the path of life; you will fill me with joy in your presence, with eternal pleasures at your right hand" (9–11).

Walking along the ocean beach hundreds of feet from the shore, you may dig a little hole in the dry sand. Soon the sand will become damp as the hole fills with water. Underneath the sand, the waters flow and fill the hole to the level of their source. Similarly, the life that is hid with Christ in God is in constant contact with the fountain of life. Though the world may not always see the overflow, the heart's depths are ever filling, and we only need to make room. Then the empty place, whether great or small, is filled to the measure of the fullness of God. This is why it is so imperative that we receive the indwelling Christ. He is the source of the river of the Water of Life. And that river flows from the throne of God. Those whose hearts are His temple can sing, no matter how the storms may rage,

> God is the Treasurer of my soul,
>   The source of lasting joy;
> A joy which time cannot impair,
>   Nor death itself destroy.

Filled with the Spirit

Be filled with the Spirit (Ephesians 5:18). You have been given fullness in Christ (Colossians 2:10).

THE EMPHATIC WORD in both verses is "filled" and "fullness." It is the Greek *plaroo*, which means to fill full—so full that there will be no space left empty. It does not mean to have a measure of the Holy Spirit and to be somewhat familiar with Christ, but to be wholly filled with, and possessed by, the Holy Spirit. It means to be utterly lost in the life and fullness of Jesus. It is the completeness of the filling that constitutes the essence of the perfect blessing. A fountain half full will never become a spring. A river half full will never become a water power. A heart half filled will never know "the peace of God which transcends all understanding" (Philippians 4:7). Neither will it know the power in the inmost being like a river flowing with living water (Psalm 1:3; John 4:14).

The nature of this filling

This filling is connected with a living Person. We are not filled with an influence, a sensation, a set of ideas and truths or a blessing. We are filled with a Person. This concept is entirely different from all other teaching. Human systems of philosophy and religion deal mainly with intellectual truths, moral conditions or external acts. Greek philosophy was a system of ideas. Confucianism is a system of morals. Judaism is a system of laws and ceremonies. Christianity is centered in a living Person, and its very essence is the indwelling life of Christ Himself. He is not only its Head and Founder but is forever its living Heart and Substance. And the Holy Spirit is simply the agent or channel through whom He enters, possesses and operates in the life consecrated to Him.

This reduces Christian life to beautiful simplicity. We do not need to fill up the various parts of our lives with many different experiences, ideas or influences. Rather, in the center of our being, we can simply receive Jesus in His personal life and fullness. Then He flows into every part of us and lives out His own life in all the diversified experiences and activities of our lives.

In one garden we plant the living seed and water it from the same great fountain, and it springs up spontaneously with all the varied beauty and fruitfulness of the lily and the rose, the foliage plant and the fruit tree, the clinging jasmine and the spreading vine. All we have to do is to turn on the fertilizing spring and nature's spontaneous life bursts forth in all its beautiful variety.

This, by a simple figure, is Christ's procedure for the deeper life. Our being is the soil, He is the Seed, His Holy Spirit is the Fountain of Living Waters and "the fruit of the Spirit is love, joy, peace, longsuffering, gentleness, goodness, faith, meekness, temperance."

Out in the West lie millions of acres of barren land. They have great potential, but practically, they are fruitless and waste. Within the soil of these deserts lie undeveloped riches, and all that is needed to bring them into fruitfulness is water. Let the mountain stream be turned into these wastes, let the irrigating channels spread their network over all these vast fields, and a lovely paradise results. The soil appears empty and barren, but fill it with seed, water it with springs, and the transformation comes with spontaneous luxuriance.

A barren possibility

So, too, the human heart is not self-constituted or self-sufficient. It is but a barren possibility. It may struggle its best to develop itself, but like the sagebrush and the stunted palms that cover the western deserts, it will develop only feebly. But drop into that heart the living Christ, and flood it with the water of the Spirit's fullness, and it realizes its true ideal. The promise of Jesus' own simple parable is perfectly fulfilled: "If a man remains in me and I in him, he will bear much fruit; apart from me you can do nothing" (John 15:5).

Shall we not realize, then, that God has made each of us, not as self-contained worlds of power and perfection, but simply as vessels waiting to be filled with Him? We are shells to hold His fullness. We are soil to receive His Living Seed and fertilizing streams, and to produce, in union with Him, the fruits of grace.

Into His living Son, God has poured all His fullness, so that "in Christ all the fullness of the Deity lives in bodily form" (Colossians 2:9). The Holy Spirit has now become the great reservoir and the irrigation system through which the fullness of Jesus flows into us.

There is nothing that God requires of us or that we can ever need in life but what Christ can supply for us. We may have an exact provision for our every need by simply receiving Him. This is the meaning of that beautiful expression, "From the fullness of his grace we have all received one blessing after another. For the law was given through Moses; grace and truth came through Jesus Christ" (John 1:16–17).

All other systems merely give us the idea of things or the commandments or laws that require them of us. But Christ brings the power to realize them. He is Himself the reality and substance in our hearts and lives. He is the great Typical Man. But He is more than a pattern or a type, exhibiting what we ought to be, demanding our imitation. He is also the Living Head and Progenitor of the life that He exhibited, producing it in each of us by an impartation of His being, reproducing Himself in us by the power of His own life. Then by the Holy Spirit from His own being, He feeds and nourishes this life in us.

Christ's Person, therefore, is far more than a pattern. He is a power, a seed, a spring of Living Water, even the substance and support of the life He requires of us.

This Person is the true fullness of every part of our life. The idea of filling implies universality and completeness. We are not filled unless we are filled in every part. This is just what Christ proposes to do in our full salvation.

He fulfills all the requirements of our salvation, all the conditions involved in connection with our redemption, reconciliation and justification. He takes the indictment against us and erases it with His own precious atonement, writing in His own blood, "Settled forever!" He takes the broken law and the sad and humiliating record of our failures, omissions and transgressions, and expunges it with His own perfect righteousness. He writes over all our record, "Christ is the end of the law so that there may be righteousness for everyone who believes" (Romans 10:4). "In love [God] predestined us to be adopted as his sons through Jesus Christ" (Ephesians 1:5). "God made him who had no sin to be sin for us, so that in him we might become the righteousness of God" (2 Corinthians 5:21).

And so we "have been given fullness in Christ" (Colossians 2:10). "By one sacrifice he has made perfect forever those who are being made holy" (Hebrews 10:14), and we are as fully saved as if we had never sinned.

A complete work

Now, the important thing is to realize that this work is complete. We should enter into the fullness of Christ by recognizing ourselves as fully justified and forever saved from all past sin and transgression through the complete redemption of Jesus Christ. The lack of fullness in our subsequent experience is largely due to doubts and limitations that we allow to enter here. Christ's work for our redemption was finished, and when we accept it, it is a complete and eternal salvation.

Christ's work fills the deeper need of sanctification. He has provided for this in His atonement and in the resources of His grace. It is wrapped up in Him and must be received as a free and perfect gift through Him alone. "You are in Christ Jesus, who has become for us wisdom from God—that is, our righteousness, holiness and redemption" (1 Corinthians 1:30).

Is sanctification the death of the sinful self? That life has been crucified with Him already upon the cross. We have but to hand it over to Him in unreserved committal, and He will slay it and bury it forever in His grave. Is sanctification a new life of purity, righteousness, peace and joy in the Holy Spirit? Still more emphatically, Christ Himself must be our life, our peace, our purity and our full and overflowing joy.

Christ is the fullness of our heart life. There is no place so sacred to us as our affections. And there is no place so claimed by Satan and so impossible to regulate by our own power and will. But Christ will give us His heart as well as His Spirit. He will cause us to love God as He loves Him—with all our "heart and with all [our] soul and with all [our] mind," (Matthew 22:38), and His love going through us will flow on to love others even as He has loved us.

Christ will also fill all the needs of our intellectual life. Our mental capacities will never know their full wealth of power and spiritual effectiveness until they become the vessels of His quickening life. These minds of ours must be laid at His feet as the censers that are to hold His holy fire. He will think in us, remember in us, judge in us. He will impart definiteness and clearness to our conceptions of truth. He will give us the tongue of fire, the illustration that both illuminates and melts, the accent and tone of persuasiveness and sympathy, the power of quick expression and utterance. He will see that we have the equipment to make us a "workman who does not need to be ashamed and who correctly handles the word of truth" (2 Timothy 2:15).

But, of course, we must be diligent and give faithful attention to His wise and holy teaching. Then as He leads us in His work, we will at once see our own shortcomings and His full purpose for us. We must be taught of God, and teaching is sometimes gradual. But "when he, the Spirit of truth, comes, he will guide [us] into all truth" (John 16:13) and will perfect those things concerning our education and preparation for His work and will. The mind that the Holy Spirit quickens and uses will accomplish results for God that all the brilliance of human genius and the scholarship of human learning can never approach.

Needs of our body

Christ will fill the needs of our body. His body has been constituted, by the resurrection from the dead, as a perpetual source of energy, sufficient for every physical function and every test that comes in the pressure of human life. In a world where every step is beset with the elements of disease, suffering and physical danger, Christ is the true life of a redeemed body. His Holy Spirit is so able to quicken these mortal bodies, as He dwells within us, that they shall receive a supernatural vigor directly derived from our exalted Head.

Christ will fill all the needs that arise in our secular callings and the circumstances of our daily lives. There is not one of them that may not be recognized as coming from Him and meant to prove His all-sufficiency in some new direction. If we had the faith to see God in every circumstance, day by day, every chapter of life's history would be a new story. The romance of heavenly love would transform darkness into light, difficulty into triumph, sorrow into joy and the earthly into the heavenly. Through us, Christ would manifest Himself in grace and power to innumerable witnesses who never hear of Him from a pulpit or read His story in the Bible.

Christ will fill our capacities for happiness. He is the fullness of our peace and joy. He is the true portion of the people He has created. Wholly filled with Him, there is no room for either care or fear.

Christ will fill that fundamental need on which every other experience of His fullness depends—the faith that receives Him. This, too, is but the life of Christ within us. Our highest part in the life of faith is to so boldly abandon even our best efforts to trust God that we can receive the faith of God and claim the promise: "everything is possible for him who believes" (Mark 9:23).

To be filled with Christ is not only to be filled with divine life in every part, but it is to be filled every moment. It is to take Him into the successive moments in our conscious existence and to abide in His fullness. Christ is not a reservoir but a spring. His life is continual, active and ever passing on with an outflow as necessary as its inflow. If we do not perpetually draw the fresh supply from the living Fountain, we will either grow stagnant or empty. It is, therefore, not so much a perpetual fullness as a perpetual filling.

True, there are periodic experiences of spiritual elation that are part of God's plan for our life in Christ and are designed, no doubt, to lift us to a higher plane of abiding union with Him. There are the Pentecosts and the second Pentecosts—the great freshets and floodtides—all of which have their necessary place in the spiritual economy. But there is the continual receiving, breath by breath and moment by moment, between those long intervals and more marked experiences. This daily supply is even more needful to spiritual steadfastness and health. God would have us alive to all His approaches and open to all the "precious dew from heaven above and . . . the deep waters that lie below; and . . . the best the sun brings forth and the finest the moon can yield; . . . the choicest gifts of the ancient mountains and the fruitfulness of the everlasting hills; . . . the best gifts of the earth and its fullness" (Deuteronomy 33:13–16). Then we will know there is no moment of existence and no part of our beings that does not draw some blessing from Him.

Effects of divine filling

This divine filling is the secret of holiness. There is a measure of the Holy Spirit's life in every regenerate soul, but it is when every part of our being is filled with His love and possessed for His glory that we are wholly sanctified. Even as the descending cloud on the tabernacle left no room for human Moses, so this divine fullness excludes from our lives the power of sin and self.

Would you have continual purity of heart and thought and feeling? Would you be entirely conformed to the will of God? "Be filled with the Spirit." "From the fullness of his grace we have all received one blessing after another" (John 1:16). Let the heavenly water flow into every channel of irrigation and by every garden bed and plant. Then the graces of your Christian life will be replenished by His grace and bloom like the garden of the Lord. Only abide in Him and let Him abide in you, and you will bring forth all the fruit of the Spirit.

This is the secret of happiness. A heart half full is only full enough to be conscious of its lack. It is when the cattle are filled that they lie down in green pastures. "These things have I spoken unto you, that my joy might remain in you, and that your joy might be full" (John 15:11, *KJV*).

It is the secret of power. The electric current can so fill a copper wire that it will become a channel to turn the great wheels of the factory. The swift river has power to run a score of factories along its banks, simply because it is perpetually supplied with water. Only full hearts accomplish effectual work for God. Only the overflow of our blessing blesses others.

Conditions for being filled

Christ has promised to fill the hungry. "Blessed are those who hunger and thirst for righteousness, for they will be filled" (Matthew 5:6). As you read these lines you may be longing for this experience and thinking with discouragement of how short you fall. This deep desire is the beginning of the blessing you seek. Already the Holy Spirit is at work preparing you for the answer to your cry. No person finds the fullness of Jesus as speedily as the one who is most deeply conscious of his or her failure and need. Thank God for that intense desire that will not let you rest short of His blessing.

An eastern caravan traveling across the desert once found itself without water. The accustomed fountains were dry and the oasis was a desert. An hour before sunset, the caravan halted, the members too exhausted and parched to continue on. Dismay was upon all faces and despair in all hearts. One of the ancient men approached the sheik and advised him to unloose the two beautiful harts he was conveying home as a present to his bride. Left to themselves, they would scour the desert for water and someone from the caravan would be able to follow them.

The animals' tongues protruded with thirst, and their bosoms heaved with distress. But as they were led out to the borders of the camp and then set free, they lifted up their heads and sniffed the air with distended nostrils. Then, with unerring instinct and a course as straight as an arrow, they sped across the desert. Several riders from the group followed close behind, and an hour or two later, they returned with the glad tidings that water had been found. With shouts of joy, the camp moved to the happily discovered fountains.

So God has put within us that instinct for the springs of living water. Thank God if you have this deep spiritual thirst for Him. Follow it as it leads you to the throne of grace to wait and cry and receive until you can say, "I am satisfied with favor and full with the blessing of the Lord."

The empty are always filled. "He has filled the hungry with good things but has sent the rich away empty" (Luke 1:53). "Blessed are those who hunger and thirst for righteousness, for they will be filled" (Matthew 5:6). "Having nothing, and yet possessing everything" (2 Corinthians 6:10). This is the paradox of grace. We never can be filled until we have room for God. Every great blessing begins with a great sacrifice, a great severance, a great dispossessing. "He brought us out . . . to bring us in" (Deuteronomy 6:23).

Abraham had to let Lot have his choice before he could have his full inheritance. Isaac had to be offered on Mount Moriah before God could make it the seat of His future temple. Moses had to let go of the honors and prospects of his Egyptian princedom before he could receive his great commission—the lasting honor of his life work. So must we be emptied of self and the world before we can be filled with Jesus and the Holy Spirit.

Are we willing to be emptied?

Are we willing to be emptied? "Make this valley full of ditches." That is the prophet's command even today; then "you will see neither wind nor rain, yet this valley will be filled with water" (2 Kings 3:16–17).

Are we in the valley of humiliation? Have we opened in the valley the deep ditches of need and conscious insufficiency? In proportion as we can say, "I am not sufficient," we will be able to add, "our competence comes from God" (2 Corinthians 3:5).

Have we tossed overboard not only the old pirate self-will and his crew of worldliness and sin but also all the cargo of our own strength, our own faith, our own religious experience? Have we made room for Christ to be our *all* and in all always? Do we habitually cease from ourselves in everything and thus make it necessary for God to assume the responsibility and supply the sufficiency?

The open heart shall be filled. God said to Israel, "Open wide your mouth and I will fill it" (Psalm 81:10). We know what it is for the flower to open its petals to the sunlight, the dew and the refreshing shower. Often we are closed so tight with unbelief, doubt, fear and self-consciousness that we cannot take in the love that God is waiting to pour out. We know what it is to find people closed up and heart-bound. We become conscious at once of the repulsion and feel all the fountains of our love obstructed and rolled back again upon our own aching hearts. They cannot receive us. It is like the mother who found her long-lost son after years of separation, but the child did not recognize her. She tried to awaken his memory of her, pouring out the full tides of her bursting heart, but her attempts only met with the dull stare of strangeness and suspicion. Her heart broken in grief and disappointment, she wept and sobbed in agony.

God is pouring out His love to many who cannot, will not receive Him. He is unknown to them. His face is strange. He seems to have no avenue to the dulled sensibilities of the world-loving man or woman. God has cause to exclaim, "How often I have longed to gather [you] together, as a hen gathers her chicks under her wings, but you were not willing" (Matthew 23:37).

I once watched a man slowly die simply because he could not swallow more than a single grain of food or spray of moisture. Many a Christian's spiritual esophagus is just as shrunken. Millions are starving to death in the midst of plenty because their hearts are not open to receive God. There must be the love that draws near and takes. There must be the faith that accepts and receives. There must be the quietness of spirit that stays open long enough to be wholly filled.

Filled by waiting

Again, we are filled by waiting upon the Lord in prayer—continued and persevering prayer. It was after His disciples had waited upon the Lord that they were filled with the Holy Spirit. Prayer is not only an asking but also a receiving. Many of us do not wait long enough before the Lord to get filled. You can take your breakfast in 15 minutes, but you cannot be filled with the Holy Spirit as quickly.

There should be seasons of special waiting upon the Lord for this purpose. There should be a ceaseless abiding in the Lord for the quiet replenishing, moment by moment. The one may be compared to the great rainstorms that flood the river, and the other to the ceaseless moisture of the air and the morning and evening dews.

No child of God who, in a proper spirit and with an entire self-surrender and trust, waits upon Him for the full baptism of His Holy Spirit will ever be disappointed. God promises that we will go forth from such seasons refreshed and overflowing with His love and life. Power and blessing will follow such seasons, both in our own life and in the lives of others. Service for God and for others is perhaps the most effectual condition of receiving continually the fullness of the Spirit. As we pour out the blessing, God will pour it in. Every blessing we have received from God is a sacred trust, and it will be continued only as we use it for Him.

Not ours but others

Our salvation is not our own. It belongs to every perishing soul in the world who has not yet had the opportunity of receiving Jesus. Our sanctification — the fullness of Jesus — is a sacred trust to be shared with every Christian who has not yet discovered this blessing. Our healing belongs to some sufferer. Our every experience is adjusted to some person and will enable us to meet his or her need if we are but faithful to the opportunities of God's providence.

How clear a truth becomes to us when we are trying to tell it to others! How real the baptism of the Holy Spirit is when we are kneeling by another's side to claim it for that one! How the streams of Christ's healing flow through our flesh as we are leading some poor sufferer into the truth! How the joy of our salvation swells as we see it spring up in the person we have just led to the fountain! What fullness God longs to share with everyone who has room to receive and readiness to give!

"If any man is thirsty, let him come to me and drink. Whoever believes in me, as the Scripture has said, streams of living water will flow from within him" (John 7:37–38). As we have received His fullness, let us pass it on, drinking as the living waters flow through our hands. Then we will realize in some measure the largeness and blessedness of that great promise of the Lord.

The Larger Life

Open wide your hearts (2 Corinthians 6:13).

T HE LAW OF GROWTH is a fundamental principle of all nature. Whatever ceases to grow begins to die. Stagnancy brings corruption; a self-contained pool becomes a swamp. Vegetation springs from a seed, the seed grows into a tree and the cycle expands into a forest. Human life commences in infancy and develops into maturity. The great plan of redemption has been a ceaseless progression and will be through the ages to come.

A starting point

The experience of the human soul is to be growth. True, it must have a starting point, for we cannot grow into Christianity. We must be born from above and then grow. Likewise, sanctification is progressive, and yet it has a definite beginning. Christ is completely formed in us, but He grows into the maturity of the perfect man in us just as He grew in His earthly life.

It is here that the enlargement of our text meets us. It is only the truly consecrated Christian who grows. The other treads the ceaseless circle of the wilderness.

The sanctified one has crossed the Jordan and begun the conquest of the land.

No book in the Bible has more progress in it than the Book of Joshua, but it only begins its highest advance when it is almost ended. It is after the whole land is subdued that the call comes: "There are still very large areas of land to be taken over" (Joshua 13:1). "How long will you wait before you begin to take possession of the land that the Lord, the God of your fathers, has given you?" (18:3). Look at old Caleb! He has the weight of 84 years on his honored head, yet he steps forward and claims the privilege of entering upon the boldest and hardest campaign of his life—the conquest of Hebron and the land of the Anakim. It is to us, then, who know the Lord Jesus in His fullness, that He is saying "Open wide your hearts!"

What it means to be enlarged

Enlargement means we need a larger vision. All great movements begin in great ideas. There is no progress without a new thought as its embryo. For 3,000 years, China remained the same because its people would not accept new ideas. Her teacher for 30 centuries was Confucius, and for those many years, there was almost no change. One cannot help but wonder what remarkable things might have occurred had the people accepted Christian truth.

The first step in our advance, then, is to secure a new concept of the truth as it is in Jesus and a larger view of His Word and His will for us. We need new eyes with which to read our Bibles and a brighter light to shine upon its deep and pregnant pages. We need to see more than a mere system of exegesis or of biblical exposition and criticism. We need to have more than a thorough knowledge of the letter and its wondrous framework of history, geography, antiquities and ancient languages. We need a vivid spiritual concept of what God is saying to us — what His thought in the Word is for each of us.

We want to take it as the message of heaven to our generation. It is the living voice of the Son of God speaking to us in this hour, and we must find in it the idea that He has for our lives and work. We must take in the promises as He reveals them for us to claim, the commandments as He intends them to be obeyed and the hopes for the future as He unfolds them for us to rejoice in!

How little we have grasped the length and breadth and depth and height of this heavenly message! How little have we realized its authority and its personal directness to us.

> Open my eyes that I may see wonderful things in your law. (Psalm 119:18)
> I keep asking that the God of our Lord Jesus Christ, the glorious Father, may give you the Spirit of wisdom and revelation, so that you may know him better. I pray also that the eyes of your heart may be enlightened in order that you may know the hope to which he has called you, the riches of his glorious inheritance in the saints and his incomparably great power for us who believe. (Ephesians 1:17–19)

We need a larger faith. What is the use of light if we do not use it? We need a faith that will personally appropriate all that we understand, a faith so large that it will reach the *fullness* of God's great promises. A faith so large that it will rise to the level of each emergency that comes into our lives. Do we not often feel that a promise has been brought to us that we have been unable to claim? Needs have risen that we know God is able to meet, but our faith is not grasping the victory, at least not according to the full measure God intends. If all things are possible to him who believes, we ought to have all things in His will for every moment of life's need. The divine pattern of faith is the faith of God.

A larger love

Still further, we need a larger love, a love that will meet God's claim of perfect love: "Love the Lord your God with all your heart and with all your soul and with all your strength and with all your mind" (Luke 10:27). We need a love that will love one another as the apostle Paul said: "Live a life of love, just as Christ loved us and gave himself up for us as a fragrant offering and sacrifice to God" (Ephesians 5:2). We need a love that will love our enemies, that will pray for those who despitefully use us and persecute us. We need a love that will love the lost as God loves them, a love that overcomes our disgust for their every repugnant condition, one that delights in suffering for their salvation—that sacrifices itself with a joy that counts it no sacrifice.

We need a love that will take our brother's need and pain as if it were our own. The love we need should reach out and "remember those in prison as if [we ourselves] were suffering" (Hebrews 13:3). We need that love of which Paul writes,

> Love is patient, love is kind. It does not envy, it does not boast, it is not proud. It is not rude, it is

not self-seeking, it is not easily angered, it keeps no record of wrongs. Love does not delight in evil but rejoices with the truth. It always protects, always trusts, always hopes, always perseveres. (1 Corinthians 13:4–7)

We need a larger joy. We need a joy that will not only rejoice in the gifts of God, but in God Himself, a joy that will find in Him our portion and our boundless and everlasting delight. We need a joy that will not only rejoice in the sunshine but in the hour of darkness. When people misunderstand us, when circumstances are against us and when even God seems to have forgotten us, that is when we need to rejoice.

We need a joy that will not only rejoice in all things but rejoice evermore. We need a joy that will "consider it pure joy" (James 1:2) and rejoice by faith, even when we do not naturally feel the joy. The joy we need should be so vast, so deep, so divine that it will not dwell on its sacrifices, will not talk about its trials. Instead, like Jesus it will, "for the joy set before him" endure the suffering and despise the shame (Hebrews 12:2).

A larger experience

Likewise, we need a larger experience. Much more than a mere state of emotional feeling, we need a larger range of Christian living, one that will bring Christ into everything. We need an experience that will prove Him in all situations. By reaching with this experience into all the circle of human life, we will say,

> I have learned to be content whatever the circumstances. I know what it is to be in need, and I know what it is to have plenty. I have learned the

> secret of being content in any and every situation, whether well fed or hungry, whether living in plenty or in want. I can do everything through him who gives me strength. (Philippians 4:11–13)

That is a large experience. That is a degree in the school of Christ that will outweigh all the doctoral degrees of all the universities.

We need a larger work, and by this we do not mean we need a larger sphere. What we need is a better quality of work. And we need to finish our unfinished work. We need to do the things that we have thought of doing, intended to do, talked about doing and are abundantly able to do. We need to do the work that can be done in the intervals and interstices of life, the work that can be done on the way and on the wing, accomplishing something *between* times as well as *in* the times of special service and appointments.

We need a work that is large in its *upward* direction, more wholly for God, more singly devoted to His glory and more satisfied with His approval, whether men are pleased or not. Furthermore, we need a larger concept and realization of the work that He expects of us in the special line in which He is developing our Christian life. We have been called to Christ in a measure unknown to the great mass of God's people. Without a doubt, we have not yet understood what God expects of us in spreading these special truths of an all-sufficient Jesus and extending this message over all the land and over all the world. God is calling us at this time to a larger faith for this special work—the testimony of Jesus in all His fullness to all the world.

We need a larger hope, realizing more vividly, more

personally, more definitely, what the coming of the Lord means to us! This needs to show up clearly in our vision so that the future will become alive with the actual expectation and ever imminent prospect of His kingdom and His reward. How little this great hope has meant to many. How utterly blind the majority of Christians have been to it as an actual experience. Great inspiration comes to the heart that truly realizes this blessed truth.

We need a larger baptism of the Holy Spirit, for this is the true summing up of all we have said. It is one thing, not many things, that we need. When we are filled with the Spirit in still larger measure, we will see the fruit of the Spirit expand and increase. We need more room for His indwelling, a wider plain for His expansion and more channels for His outflow. We are not limited in Him; we are limited in ourselves. "God gives the Spirit without limit" (John 3:34), but we receive Him in confined and small capacities. He wants our entire being, and He wants to so fill it that we will be expanded into larger possibilities for His inworking and His outflowing.

Let us "Open wide [our] hearts," not only in all these senses and directions but also in the quality of our lives. We want not only more breadth and length, but we want depth and height. Let us seek to be more spiritual, more mellow, more mature, more fruitful and more established, settled and immovable as we stand in and for Him.

Entering into this life of enlargement

In order to be enlarged, we must be delivered from and lifted above our old concepts, ideas and experiences. In a word, we must be delivered from our past.

Old things must pass away before all things can be made new. We must die to our religious self as well as to our sinful self. It was when he was far on in the spiritual life that Paul uttered that sublime aspiration: "Forgetting what is behind and straining toward what is ahead, I press on toward the goal to win the prize for which God has called me heavenward in Christ Jesus" (Philippians 4:13–14).

In the various strata of earth, we find traces of the wreck of early organic life. There was a creation and then there was a disintegration, and on its ruins a new and higher development occurred. So in the spiritual world, we come to the place where we are conscious that the old experience fails to satisfy. The old "Rephidims" are dry, and we must open some new rock of Horeb and receive supplies from a higher source than before.

Let the old things pass away. They are but the basis of something better. Let the old turnpike be broken up. The King's highway is to be built on top of it!

There is nothing that keeps us from advancement more than ruts—the wheel tracks in which our chariots roll with unchanging monotony. Life's currents carry us in the same old direction until the law of habit makes a new tack almost impossible. The true remedy for all this is to commence each day anew, and commence at nothing. Take Christ afresh to be the Alpha and Omega of all your experiences. Wait even for His concept of thought, desire and prayer, fearing only that your highest thought would be below His great plan of wisdom and love.

Are you trying to get back an old experience? If you were to succeed in this, you would only be where you once were. If you are only going to get where you once were, then you have abandoned the law of progress and begun the downward retrogression. God Himself has withered the flower and fragrance of your former joys so that He may lead you into something better! Let your old experience go, and take the living, everlasting Christ instead. Be willing to be enlarged according to His thought, and He will do exceeding abundantly above all that you have yet been able to ask or think.

God's divine ideal

If we would be enlarged according to the thought of God, we must be delivered from all human standards, opinions and patterns and accept nothing less than God's own divine ideal. Multitudes are kept from spiritual progress by cast-iron systems of doctrine that have settled forever the idea that holiness is possible in the present life. Such people would declare that no mere man, since the Fall, is able to keep the commandments of God without breaking them daily in word, thought and deed. And then a row of human characters is set before us to prove the impossibility of sanctification and to show the satisfying and humbling influence of human imperfection. They have made up their minds in advance that they can never have the fullness of Jesus beyond certain narrow limits, and of course they cannot advance beyond the standards they set up!

We do agree with the idea that no mere man can be holy or blameless, but the Lord Jesus is no mere man. When He owns and keeps the heart, He does so with *His* holiness and divine keeping. We assert that what no mere man can do, the living Christ can do and does do for those who abide in Him! Let us take the divine measure, whatever men may think or say.

Many people are also looking constantly to some human example and "when they measure themselves by themselves and compare themselves with themselves, they are not wise" (2 Corinthians 10:12). Either we will find ourselves as good as someone else and be content, or we will be satisfied to be similar to some human ideal and stop short of the only perfect pattern, Christ Himself.

We will never grow up to the measure of the Lord until we take the Lord's own word and character as our standard and ideal. We must take our stand upon the sure and immutable ground that He who is holy commands us to be holy. He who promises His own grace and all-sufficiency, enabling us to meet those demands, will not excuse us if we fail. He has offered us Himself as the life and power to be obedient and to be holy, and nothing less than his own perfect example should ever satisfy our holy ambition! Looking unto Him, pressing ever closer to His side and following in His footprints, we will be transformed into the same image, from glory to glory, and will thus go from one level of strength to another.

Accepting what He sends

If we would be enlarged, we must accept all that God sends us to develop and expand our spiritual life. We are so content to abide at the old level that God often has to compel us to rise higher by bringing us face to face with situations that we cannot meet without much greater measures of His grace. It is as though He had to send a tidal wave to flood the lowlands where we dwell to compel us to move into the hills beyond. God, like the mother bird, sometimes has to break up the comfortable, downy nest, letting us drop into empty space. There we must either learn to use an entirely new and higher method of support or sink into failure and loss. We must do or die, fly or fall to our destruction.

In this way, God allowed the crisis of His terrible peril to close in around Jacob one night. There, as he bowed at Peniel in supplication, God brought Jacob to the place where he could take hold of God as he would never have done otherwise. And from that narrow passageway through the peril, Jacob came forth enlarged in his faith and in his knowledge of God. He had the power of a new and victorious life!

God had to let Israel be shut in at the Red Sea so that they might be compelled to take hold of God for their supernatural help. It was either that or die. God had to compel David by a long and painful discipline that lasted for years, to teach him His almighty power and faithfulness. By this God taught him to grow up into the established principles of faith and godliness that were indispensable for his subsequent and glorious career as king of Israel.

Look at Paul. Nothing but the extremities in which he was constantly placed could have ever taught him—and taught the churches through him—the full meaning of the great promise he so wonderfully learned to claim: "My grace is sufficient for you" (2 Corinthians 12:9). Nothing but our trials and perils would ever have led some of us to know Him as we do, to trust Him as we have and to draw from Him the measures of grace that our extremities made indispensable.

Often God calls us to work far beyond our natural

strength or endowments. But the emergency throws us upon Him, and we always find Him more than equal to the need that His wisdom and providence have brought into our way.

Many of us can remember how in the beginning of our Christian work we ventured to accept positions of responsibility for which we felt we were inadequate. But as we threw ourselves upon God and dared to go forward, His grace proved to be sufficient.

When I was a young minister, 21 years of age and just leaving theological seminary, I had the choice of two fields of labor. One was an extremely easy one. It was a refined, friendly, prosperous church in a delightful town, just large enough to be an ideal field for one who wished to spend a few years in quiet preparation for future usefulness. The other was a large, absorbing city church with many hundreds of members and with heavy, overwhelming burdens. This church was sure to demand the utmost possible care, labor and responsibility.

All my friends, teachers and counselors advised me to take the easier place. But I felt an impulse, which must have had some human ambition in it, that I now believe to have been at least indirectly a guidance from God. I felt that if I took the easier place, I would probably rise to meet that challenge and no more. But if I took the harder place, I would not rest short of all its requirements. That is exactly how I found it to be. My early ministry was developed and the habit of venturing into difficult undertakings was largely established, by the grace of God, through the necessities of this difficult position.

Let us, then, be willing to be enlarged, although it

may involve many a sacrifice, many a peril and many a hazardous undertaking.

Let the Spirit work

If we would be enlarged, let us take the Holy Spirit Himself to enlarge us by filling us with His fullness. The highest enlargement is by the power of expansion. It is the incoming wave that enlarges the little pool as it fills it and then rolls back to the sea to return with still larger fullness and make yet ampler room. Nothing so thoroughly sweeps away the littleness of our concepts of God, the pettiness of our faith or the narrowness of our love, like a steady gaze into His face! Feel the tides of His love and be thrilled with the touch of His own heart and its mighty purposes for us and for the world for which He died. That will deal with all the meanness of our self-consciousness and the insignificance of our work, and we will find all our delight in the glory of His presence.

We hardly need to say that the place to receive Him is the mercy seat. Waiting before Him in prayer, receiving Him in communion, drinking deeper and deeper of His life and love, the vessel is not only filled but expanded. Then we will know something of the power of the apostle's prayer,

> That out of his glorious riches he may strengthen you with power through his Spirit in your inner being, so that Christ may dwell in your hearts through faith. And I pray that you, being rooted and established in love, may have power together with all the saints, to grasp how wide and long and high and deep is the love of Christ, and to know this love that surpasses knowledge—that

you may be filled to the measure of all the fullness of God. (Ephesians 3:16–19)

If we would be enlarged to the full measure of God's purpose, let us endeavor to realize something of our own capacities for His filling. We little know the size of the human soul and spirit. Never, until He renews, cleanses and enters the heart, can we have any adequate concept of the possibilities ahead. But we can take comfort in knowing that we are made in His image, and He will renew us after the pattern of the Lord Jesus Himself.

When we remember that God has made the human soul to be His temple and abode, we can be sure that there are capacities in the human spirit that none of us has ever yet begun to realize! We know something of them as we experience the coming of the Holy Spirit. Then, from time to time, new baptisms awaken the dormant powers and susceptibilities that we did not know we possessed.

All this is only the beginning of an infinite possibility. God sometimes takes a low, coarse, brutal nature, which for years has seemed to possess capacity only for crime and sensuality, and makes it not only as pure but as bright as an angel's mind! Only God could take such a brain, voice, tongue, taste or imagination and so powerfully illuminate and vivify it and make it to be gloriously fruitful. Yet we see this work of God manifested in the transformed life of the allegorist John Bunyan and in the utterly changed behavior of the exquisite hymnwriter, John Newton.

Let us, then, give God the right to make the best of us, and someday, filled with wonder, we will behold the glorious temple He has reared and say, "Lord, what is man that you are mindful of him?" (Psalm 8:4).

God's magnitude

If we would rise to the full measure of God's standard for us, let us realize the magnitude of God as well as the magnitude of our own being. It is with nothing less than Himself that He means to fill us. Take in the full dimensions of His resources of grace: its length, breadth, depth and height. Then, let us measure if we can the magnitude of God who is the living substance and personal source of all grace. Only then can we have some approximation of what the apostle means when he exclaims, "Now to him who is able to do immeasurably more than all we ask or imagine, according to his power that is at work within us, to him be glory in the church and in Christ Jesus throughout all generations, for ever and ever! Amen" (Ephesians 3:20–21).

Last of all, let us remember that we have eternal years in which to develop all this divine ideal. If we could just see ourselves as we some day will be! If only we could behold that glorious creature God shall make of us in His holy image! Could we but see our faces as they shall be—shining like the sun in the kingdom of our Father—and hear the songs of rapture that shall burst from our lips in higher notes than angels ever sang. If only we could see all things, we would wonder at the smallness of our faith today when we fear to ask our Father for the merest fraction of advance on our great inheritance!

This is no figment of the imagination. It is no soaring dream of hope or fancy. God has told us plainly that "we shall be like Him" when He appears (1 John

3:2). If only we could enter heaven now and gaze for a moment on the glorious face of Jesus, "like the shining sun in all its brilliance" (Revelation 1:16). If we could comprehend the infinite wisdom that even now is taking in the whole sweep of the universe in the grasp of His thought. If we could understand in some way His infinite ability to listen to a thousand prayers at once, then we would not hesitate to ask Him for great things!

If we could watch as He administrates the government of innumerable worlds and yet takes the time to hear our faintest cry. If we could measure His omnipotence as He holds in His hands the controls of universal power and dominion. If we could stand the breathtaking vision of His beauty and feel the thrill of His love in all its ecstatic power, we would, to some degree, see something of what we ourselves are yet to be.

Think of it! "Then [we] shall know fully, even as [we are] fully known" (1 Corinthians 13:12). We will share the work of His omnipotence. We will shine in His beauty. We will reflect His moral perfections. We will sit with Him on His throne. We will be invested with His transcendent glory. And all we receive of Him today is a mere installment in advance of that which is already our own by right of inheritance. Yet this is *all* ours and can be actually realized as fast as we can take it in!

We have eternity before us. Let us rise up to the height of such a prospect even here. Let us walk as those who dwell in heavenly places and share the resurrection and ascension life of our living Head!

Rise with your risen Lord,
Ascend with Christ above,

And in the heavenlies walk with Him
  Whom seeing not, you love.

Look on your trials here
  As He beholds them now;
Look on this world as it will seem
  When glory crowns your brow.

Walk as a heavenly race,
  Princes of royal blood;
Walk as the children of the Lord,
  The sons and heirs of God.

Fear not to take your place
  With Jesus on the throne,
And bid the pow'rs of earth and hell;
  His sovereign sceptre own.

Your full redemption rights
  With holy boldness claim;
And to its utmost fullness prove
  The pow'r of Jesus' name!

Your life is hidden now,
  Your glory none can see,
But when He comes His bride shall shine,
  All glorious as He!

Death to Self

I no longer live, but Christ lives in me (Galatians 2:20).

THE STORY OF ABRAHAM, ISHMAEL AND ISAAC is a parable illustrating this text. The casting out of Ishmael, according to Galatians 4:24, is an allegory expressing a spiritual truth. It speaks of the spiritual experience of the believer when he dies to the law and to sin through the cross of Jesus Christ.

There is, however, something more in this account than our deliverance from the power of indwelling sin. In the patriarchal story, this deliverance was followed by the offering up of Isaac on Mount Moriah. There can be no doubt what this signifies: the deeper spiritual experience into which the fully consecrated person must come. In this act of obedience, the sanctified self is laid on the altar just as Isaac was. Thus, from that point on, we become dead not only to sin but to that which is worse than sin — self.

> There is a foe whose hidden power
>   The Christian well may fear;
> More subtle far than inbred sin,
>   And to the heart more dear.
> It is the power of selfishness,
>   The proud and willful I;

And e'er my Lord can live in me,
My very self must die.

This is the lesson of Isaac's offering and Paul's experience. "I have been crucified with Christ and I no longer live"—that is the death of sin. "But Christ lives in me"—that is the offering of Isaac, the deliverance from self and even the substitution of Christ Himself for the new self. This is a substitution so complete that the faith by which this life is maintained is no longer our self-sustained confidence but the "faith [of] the Son of God, who loved [us] and gave himself for [us]" (Galatians 2:20). Thus He is our Substitute.

The forms of self

In the Book of Joshua, we read of the three sons of Anak—a race of giants who held the city of Hebron before Caleb's conquest and were the terror of the Israelites. The name Anak literally means long-necked, and for our purposes, we can compare the name to pride, confidence, willfulness and self-sufficiency.

The first of the Anakites may be called Self-will, the disposition to rule and especially to rule ourselves. It is the spirit that brooks no other will and is its own law and god. The first step in the consecrated life, therefore, is unconditional surrender to God. Breaking the power of self cannot be done without doing this. And only this will establish forever the absolute sovereignty of the will of God in the heart and life of the Christian.

We cannot abide in holiness or be wholly used by God until self-will is crucified. We must be so totally crucified that we would not even think of acting contrary to God's will or orders. This is obedience, and obedience is the law of the Christian life. It must be absolute, unquestioning and without any possible exception. "You are my friends if you do what I command" (John 15:14).

In the life of faith, God requires us to exercise a strong will continually. There is no doubt that faith itself is largely the exercise of a sanctified and intensified will. But in order to do this, our will must be wholly renounced, and God's will invariably accepted in its place. Then we can put into it all the strength and force of our being and will *what* God wills, *as* He wills it and *because* He wills it. In short, it is an exchanged will. The despotic tyranny of Anak is exchanged for the wise, beneficent sovereignty of God.

Self-confidence is the next of Anak's race. It is the spirit that draws its strength from self alone and disdains the arm of God and the help of His grace. In a milder form, it is the spirit that trusts its own spiritual graces or virtues, its own morality, courage, faith, purity and steadfastness, its own joy and transitory emotions of hope, enthusiasm and zeal. It is just as necessary to die to our self-sufficiency as to our self-will. If we do not, we will experience failure after failure until we learn what others have learned—that we are not competent in ourselves to overcome (2 Corinthians 3:5), because "our competence comes from God."

The sanctified heart is not a self-constituted engine of power. It is a set of wheels and gears that are absolutely and continually dependent upon the powerful engine itself to make them move! It is a capacity to hold God—a vessel to be filled with His goodness, held and used by His hand. The sanctified life is a possibility of which He, by His abiding fullness, is constantly the motivating power and the impelling force. The word *consecrate* in Hebrew means "to fill the hand." This beautiful definition suggests the idea of an empty hand that God Himself must continually fill.

Self-glorying is the last and most impious of the race. He takes the throne of Jehovah and claims the glory due unto Him alone. Sometimes its form is a desire for human praise. Sometimes it is a pride so subtle that it will not stoop to care about the approval of others. Its supreme delight is in its own self-consciousness and superiority, ability or goodness.

There are those who say vanity is a vice inferior to pride. Vanity only seeks the praise of others, but pride disdains the opinions of others and rests back in the complacent consciousness of its own excellence. Whatever its phase may be, the root and principle are the same. It is impious self, sitting on the throne of God, claiming the honor and glory that belong to Him alone.

Biblical illustrations

These three forms of self are illustrated by three examples in the Word of God. Saul, the first king of Israel, is a fearful monument to the peril of self-will. His downward career began in a single act of disobedience. Although his disobedience seemed to be merely a question of detail, it was really an act of self-will. He was making a substitution of his own choice in place of God's express command.

The prophet, Samuel, characterizes his sin in these expressive words: "To obey is better than sacrifice, and to heed is better than the fat of rams. For rebellion is like the sin of divination, and arrogance like the evil of idolatry. Because you have rejected the word of the Lord, he has rejected you as king" (1 Samuel 15:22–23).

It is evident that the essence of Saul's sin lay in this element of willfulness and stubbornness. He had dared to substitute his own ideas and preferences for the word of Jehovah. From this moment on, his obedience was necessarily qualified and, of course, worthless. God then sent His prophet to choose a different king who, although full of human imperfections, had this one thing on which God could fully depend: he had a purpose to obey God when he understood His will! For that reason, God says of David, "I have found David son of Jesse a man after my own heart; he will do everything I want him to do" (Acts 13:22).

David made many mistakes and committed dark and terrible sins, but they were done when he was under strong temptation and blinded by passion and haste. Never did he do it with the deliberate purpose of disobeying God. The sad story of Saul's downward descent and final, tragic ruin should be enough to make us tremble at the peril that lies before any willful person! May it ever cause us to cry out, "My Father, not as I will, but as you will" (Matthew 26:39).

The peril of self-confidence is seen just as markedly in Simon Peter. Strong in his transitory enthusiasm and ignorant of his own heart's weakness, he honestly meant what he said to the Lord: "Even if all fall away on account of you, I never will" (Matthew 26:33). But, sadly, there came the shameful denial, the piercing look of Jesus, the bitter tears of penitence and the awful hours of the crucifixion. These all taught Peter the lesson of his nothingness and the necessity of walking no longer in self-confidence but humbly, in the strength of the Lord alone!

We are given a vivid and impressive object lesson of the last form of self-will—the pride that glories in its own achievements and excellencies—in the account of Nebuchadnezzar. "Is not this the great Babylon I have built?" he cries in the hour of his triumph (Daniel 4:30). As he looked upon the city, surely he saw that it was indeed a paragon of human glory, the metropolis of his mighty empire that literally included the world.

If mortal man ever had a reason to glory in earthly magnificence, Nebuchadnezzar had it. After all, God Himself had compared him and his kingdom to a majestic head of gold and had symbolized his power as a winged lion. But the instant that vainglorious word reached the ears of God, the answer fell from heaven like a knell of judgment: "Your royal authority has been taken away from you. You will be driven away from people and will live with the wild animals; you will eat grass like cattle. Seven times will pass by for you until you acknowledge that the Most High is Sovereign over the kingdoms of men and gives them to anyone he wishes" (Daniel 4:30–32).

Follower of God beware!

This is the glorying of the carnal heart. But beware! The follower of God may mingle his own self-seeking and his own honor with his work for God and thus impair his usefulness and lose his reward.

Such was the case of Jonah. There is no picture that is more pitiful than that of the morbid and grumbling prophet who sat outside of Nineveh. He sat under a withered gourd, his face blistered and swollen with the scorching sun and his eyes red from useless weeping. Hear him asking God to let him die because his ministry had been dishonored. He presented a spectacle of ridiculous melancholy and chagrin while all around him millions were rejoicing, praising God for His mercy in delivering them from an awful catastrophe. Poor Jonah!

God had given him the most honorable ministry ever accorded to a human being — he was called to be the first foreign missionary. He had been sent to preach to the mightiest empire on the face of the globe, the imperial city of the world — proud Ninevah. His preaching had been successful as no mortal had ever known success. The whole city was lying prostrate on their faces at the footstool of mercy. With penitence and prayer, the nation's hearts, for the moment at least, were turned to God.

In spite of all this, Jonah was full of himself over the work he had done and utterly absorbed in his own credit, reputation and honor. God had listened to the penitential cries of the Ninevites and had revoked the sentence that Jonah himself had uttered. This rendered his prophecy null and void. Jonah was afraid that afterward, he would be ridiculed as a fanatic and an idle alarmist. Disgusted and exasperated, he acted like a spoiled child, throwing himself on the ground and asking God to kill him. He did all this just because God had, by His mercy, spoiled his reputation as a true prophet. Jonah could not see, as God did, the unspeakable horror and anguish that had been averted.

The prophet could not see the joy of the divine heart in exercising mercy and in hearing the penitent

cries of the people. He could not see the great principle of grace that underlies the divine threatenings. He
could not understand that great-souled pity that felt
for the one hundred thousand infant children of that
great capital who would have moaned in their dying
agony if Nineveh had fallen.

All he thought about was his own reputation as
a prophet and what people might say when they
learned his word had not come to pass. With that one
little worm gnawing at the root, his peace and happiness, like his own gourd, withered away. So God had
to set him up as a dried specimen of selfishness, to
show others the meanness and misery the self-life can
bring to a person who tries to mingle his or her own
glory with the sacred word of the glorious God.

This worm self has rendered it impossible for God
to use many a gifted man or woman. It has blighted
the church of Christ and rendered vain the ministry of
thousands, because God could not use them without
giving to them the glory that He will never give to
another.

God knew the secret bane of Jonah's heart—that
was why he immersed him for three days and nights
in the stomach of a fish. Out of that experience Jonah
came—as a great many other people come out of the
experience of sanctification—with a big self, supreme
even in the sin-cleansed soul. Let us therefore lift up
the earnest prayer:

> Oh, to be saved from myself, dear Lord:
>   Oh, to be lost in Thee!
> Oh that it might be no more I,
>   But Christ who lives in me!

The effects of self

Self dishonors God and sets up a rival on His throne. The devil was not altogether a liar when he said to our first parents, "You will be like God" (Genesis 3:5). This is just what fallen man tries to be, a god unto himself. This is the essence of the sin of selfishness, for it puts man in the place of God by making him a law and an end unto himself.

Whenever a person acts for his own selfish will or self-interest purely as an end, he is claiming to be his own god, and he is directly disobeying the first commandment: "You shall have no other gods before me" (Exodus 20:3). Moreover, in assuming the place of God, he is doing it in a spirit completely contrary to God's Spirit. God is love, and love is the opposite of selfishness. He is thus mocking God and, at the same time, proving his utter unfitness to occupy His throne by his unlikeness of Him.

Self also leads to every other sin and brings back the power of the carnal life. Self alone attempts to keep the heart, but it finds sin and Satan too strong. Self-perfection is not possible for any man. There must be more than "I" before there can be victory.

In Romans 7:15, Paul tells us what "I" can do. It can only struggle ineffectively. In the next chapter (8:10), he points the way to triumph and victory. The man or woman who goes only far enough to receive Adamic purity, if such a thing is really included in the gospel, will soon have the next chapter of Adamic history, and that is the temptation and fall. But the person who receives Christ to dwell within and to keep the heart by His mighty power, shall rise "to the fullness of Christ" (Ephesians 4:13).

Still further, the self-life leads back to the dominion of Satan. Satan's own fall probably began in the form of self-love. Made to be dependent on God every moment, he desired independence. Contemplating his own perfection and thinking it was something that was his own, he became separated from God and fell into rebellion against Him. This led to eternal rivalry, disobedience and all that can be opposite to the divine and holy.

Any person who becomes self-constituted or occupied with his or her own virtues and tries to be independent of Jesus will fall under the power of Satan and share his awful descent. Jesus must be our source of strength and the supreme end of our being.

Self is likewise fatal to the spirit of love and harmony. It is the source of strife, bigotry, suspicion, sectarianism, envy, jealousy and the whole race of social sins and grievances that afflict the Christian life and the church of God. It is the mother of division from the beginning. Where it prevails, there can be no true unity, no happy cooperation. There can never be a harmonious church or a happy family where self is predominant in the hearts of the people. The secret of Christian cooperation and happy church life is "bearing with one another in love," making "every effort to keep the unity of the Spirit through the bond of peace" (Ephesians 4:2–3) and learning to "honor one another above yourselves" (Romans 12:10).

Self mars our work for God

Self-will mars our work for God and tries to force the chariots of God's power and grace upon our own sidetracks. And God will never permit that. Self-confidence seeks to build up the kingdom of Christ by human ability and unsanctified instrumentalities and presumes to go where God has not sent us and to do what He has not qualified us to do. The result is but a crude work, defiled by worldliness and sin, impermanent and unfruitful. Much of today's Christian work is of this nature.

The spirit of self-glorying will try to use the pulpit, the choir loft, the religious paper, the charitable scheme and even the mission of winning souls as a channel for magnifying a personality or successful worker or by glorifying some rich donor. God is disgusted with the spirit of idolatry. Until we are so yielded to our Master that He and He alone can be glorified in our work, the Lord cannot trust us with much service for Him.

Self makes us unhappy. It is a root of bitterness in every heart where it reigns. The secret of joy is hidden in the heart of love, and the arms of self are too short to ever reach it. Until we dwell in God and God dwells in us, until we learn to find happiness in being lost in Him, living for His glory and for His people, we will never taste the sweets of divine blessedness.

Only running water is living water, and only when it is poured into other vessels does it become wine. The self-willed man is always a miserable person. He gets his own way and does not enjoy it. After he has it, he wishes he had never got it, because it usually leads him over a precipice. The self-sufficient man can never know the springs that lie outside his own little heart. And the self-glorying man, like Herod, is eaten by the worms of corruption and remorse that always feed upon the impious person who dares to claim the honors due to God alone.

Then too, self-love always leads to a fall. The boasted wisdom must be proved to be foolishness. The proud arm must be laid, as Pharaoh's, in the dust. The self-sufficient boast, such as the one Peter made, must be answered by its own failure. The disobedient path that refuses God's wise and holy will must be proved to be a false way. Every idol must be abolished, every high thing brought low; no flesh may glory in His presence.

Let us ask our faithful God to save us from this tyrant self that dishonors God, that leads us into captivity to Satan, withers love, mars the work of God, poisons all our happiness and plunges us into failure and ruin. Let us ask Him to show us that we are nothing, and then we will be glad to have Christ live in us—He who "fills everything in every way" (Ephesians 1:23).

The remedy for self

God has often let self have its way until it cures us effectually by showing us the misery and failure that it brings. This is the only good there is in our own struggling. It shows us the vanity of the struggle and prepares us to surrender to God. But let us beware how much we assert ourselves, because there is always one step too far that will prevent us from ever returning.

God has placed around us also the restraints of other hearts and lives as checks upon our selfishness. They are like links that almost compel us to reach beyond ourselves and to work with and live for others. He has made no man independent of his brothers. "In him the whole building is joined together" (Ephesians 2:21), and we grow together into a holy temple in the Lord. We are adjusted, bone to His bone, and by that which every joint supplies, the body is ministered to and grows into the fullness of His stature.

The church of Christ is no autocracy where one man can be a dictator or judge, but a fellowship where One alone is Master. Any work that develops into a one-man despotism withers. It is true that God has ranks of workers, but they are all harmonious and linked in heavenly love. The man who cannot work with his brothers in mutual comfort and harmony has something yet to learn in his own Christian life.

While God will teach any of us by ourselves and wants us to be independent of our fellow Christians in the sense of leaning on them instead of God, He does require that we should be able to cooperate with them. It is our God-given responsibility to submit ourselves one to another in the fear of God. One may sow and another reap, but both will rejoice together as they "carry each other's burdens, and in this way . . . fulfill the law of Christ" (Galatians 6:2) as true yokefellows (Philippians 4:3).

The love of Jesus is the divinely appointed prescription for the death of self. Paul expresses this in Second Corinthians: "One died for all, and therefore all died. And he died for all, that those who live should no longer live for themselves but for him who died for them and was raised again" (5:14).

That is the simple story of the death of self in the Christian life. It is the love of Jesus that has excluded it, and never, until we become fascinated by His affection and captivated by His love, will we cease to live for ourselves. But then, we will toil and suffer with Him and follow Him anywhere. If we would die to self, we must fall in love with Jesus. Only then will we be content without the many things that before we thought we must have. Our hearts will be so satisfied with Him that we cannot speak or even think of it as sacrifice or suffering. Now His smile is our sunshine, His presence is our joy and His love is our heaven!

But it is not only the love of Christ that we want— it is the living Christ Himself. Many people have touches of the love of Christ, but for them He is a Christ far removed. The apostle Paul speaks of something far greater. It is Christ Himself who lives inside and who is big enough to crowd out and keep out the little "I." There is no other who can truly lift and keep the heart above the power of self but Jesus. He is the Mighty Lord, stronger than the armed strong man.

Blessed Christ! He is able not only for sin, sorrow and sickness, but He is able for you and me personally. He is able to so be our life, that moment by moment we will be conscious that He is filling us with Himself and conquering the self that ruled us before. The more we try to fight self, the more it clings to us. But that moment we turn away from it and look to Christ, He fills all the consciousness and disperses everything with His own presence. Let us abide in Him and we will find there is nothing else to do.

The Spirit's work

It is almost the same thing, but another way of saying it, that the baptism and indwelling of the Holy Spirit will deliver and keep us from the power of self. When the cloud of glory entered the tabernacle, there was no room for Moses to remain. And when filled with the heavenly presence of the blessed Spirit, we are lost in God and self hides away. Like Job we can say, "My ears have heard of you, but now my eyes have seen you. Therefore I despise myself and repent in dust and ashes" (Job 42:5–6).

These bodies of ours were made for Him. Let Him fill them so completely that we will be like the oriental temple of glass in the ancient legend. When the sun shone on it, the temple was not seen. The observer could only behold the glorious sunlight that it reflected. The transparent walls were all but unnoticed.

That all the things God has used have first been sacrificed is not a new thought but an appropriate one. We have a sacrificed Savior who emptied Himself, making Himself of no reputation. "Therefore God exalted him to the highest place and gave him the name that is above every name, that at the name of Jesus every knee should bow, in heaven and on earth and under the earth" (Philippians 2:9). It was a sacrificed Isaac whom God made the promised seed and progenitor of Israel's tribes. And it was on Mount Moriah where God afterward raised up His glorious temple. Even so, it is only when our Isaac is on the altar and our whole being is lost in God that He can lay the deep foundations and rear the everlasting walls of the living temple in which He is the supreme and eternal glory.

I look back today with unutterable gratitude to the lonely and sorrowful night when, mistaken in many things and imperfect in all, my heart's first full consecration was made. I did not know but what it would be death in the most literal sense before the morning light, yet with unreserved surrender I could say,

Jesus, I my cross have taken,
    All to leave and follow thee;

> Destitute, despised, forsaken,
>   Thou from hence my All shalt be.

Never before had my heart known quite such a thrill of joy as when, on the following Sunday morning, I gave out those lines and sang them with all my heart. And if God has been pleased to make my life in any measure a little temple for His indwelling and for His glory, it has been because of that hour—the keynote of a consecrated, crucified and Christ-devoted life.

Come, fellow Christian, and let Him teach you the superlative degree of joy. This is the joy that has learned to say not only "My lover is mine" but even better, "I am his" (Song of Solomon 2:16).

More Than Conquerors

In all these things we are more than conquerors through him who loved us (Romans 8:37).

IT IS A GREAT THING to be a conqueror in Christian life and conflict. It is a much greater thing to be a conqueror "in all these things" the apostle names—a great host of trials, troubles and woes. But what does it mean to be "more than conqueror"?

It means a person will have a decisive victory. There are some victories that cost nearly as much as defeats, and for us to endure more than a few of such victories would surely destroy us. There are some battles that have to be fought again and again, and we become exhausted with ceaseless strife. Many Christians are kept in constant warfare, because they lack the courage to venture into a bold and final contest to end the strife by a decisive victory. It is a blessing to so die that we are dead indeed to sin. Real joy comes when we completely sever that last strand of our reluctance to obey God. True peace will never come until we say such an absolute *no* to the enemy that he will never repeat the solicitation.

There are, in this world's history, battles that are so decisive that they settle the future of an empire or of a world. We have such battles too. But God is able to give us the grace to so win in a few encounters that there will be no doubt about the side on which the victory falls, and there is no danger of the contest ever being renewed. Other battles we may have and will have. But surely it is possible for us to settle the questions that meet us, one by one, and settle them forever.

Have you been weakened by your indecisiveness in your views of truth, in your steps of faith, in your refusals of temptation, in your surrender to God, in your consecration to His service and obedience to His special call? Perhaps you have been uncertain enough to keep the question open and tempt the adversary to continue to press the conflict. We read in God's Word after Joshua's bold triumphs or David's well-fought battles: "Then the land had rest from war" (Joshua 14:15), "The Lord had given him rest from all his enemies" (2 Samuel 7:1). In the same way, we will have rest by becoming "more than conquerors through him who loved us."

Breaking the enemy's power

To be more than conqueror means that we may have such complete victory that it will eventually break the adversary's power. It will not only defend us from his attacks but effectively weaken and destroy his strength. This is one of the purposes of temptation. We can work together with God in destroying evil. Of Joshua's battles we read that "It was the Lord himself who hardened their hearts to wage war against Israel, so that he might destroy them totally" (Joshua 11:20). It was not enough for Israel to beat them off and be saved from their attacks. God wanted them exterminated.

In like manner, when God allows the enemy to

appear in our lives, it is that we may do him irreparable and eternal injury, thus glorifying God! For this purpose, God frequently brings to light in our own lives evils that were concealed, not that they might crush us, but that we might put them out of the way. If not for their discovery and resistance, they might continue to be hidden and some day break out with fatal effectiveness. God allows them to be provoked into action in order to challenge our resistance and lead us into an aggressive and victorious advance against them.

When we find anything in our hearts and lives that seems to threaten our triumph or His work, let us remember this: God has allowed it to confront us so that in His name, we might forever put it aside and render it powerless to injure and oppose us again.

Are we thus fighting the good fight of faith? Are we resisting the devil and rising up for God against those who oppose God? Do we look upon our adversaries and obstacles as things that have come to crush us? Or do we see them as things to be put aside, things that will become tributary to our successes and our Master's glory? If so, we will be "more than conquerors through him who loved us." Then, as Isaiah expressed it, "All who rage against you will surely be ashamed and disgraced; those who oppose you will be as nothing and perish. Though you search for your enemies, you will not find them. Those who wage war against you will be as nothing at all" (Isaiah 41:11–12).

To be more than conqueror means also that we will have such a victory that the battle will bring us benefits and contribute to our own and the Master's cause. It is possible, in a certain sense, to take our enemies as prisoners and make them fight in our ranks, or at least to do the menial work of our camp. Similarly, it is possible to get such good out of Satan's assaults that he will actually, though unintentionally, become our ally. Then, to his eternal chagrin, he will find that he has actually been doing us some real service.

Doubtless, he thought that when he stirred up Pharaoh to murder the little Hebrew children he was exterminating the race he so feared. But that act brought Moses into Pharaoh's house and raised up a deliverer for Israel who would destroy Pharaoh. Surely that was being "more than conqueror!" Again, Satan overmatched himself when he instigated Haman to build his lofty gallows and then send forth the decree for Israel's extermination. He had the misery of seeing Haman hang on those same gallows and Israel utterly delivered.

No doubt he put the Hebrew children into the blazing furnace and Daniel into the den of lions thinking he had destroyed the last remnant of godliness on the earth. But no, these heroes were "more than conquerors!" Not only did they escape their destroyer, but their deliverance led to Nebuchadnezzar's proclamation that magnified the truth of God through the entire Babylonian empire. In a similar way, Darius was prompted to recognize God throughout all the regions of the still greater Persian empire.

Satan's most audacious attempt was in the crucifixion of our Lord, and all hell, no doubt, held high jubilee on that dark afternoon when Jesus sank into death. But wait! The cross became the weapon by which Satan's head was bruised and by which his kingdom will yet be exterminated. God makes him forge the very weapons of his own destruction and hurl thunderbolts that will fall back upon his own head. In like manner, we may thus turn his fiercest assaults to our own advantage and to the glory of our King!

Two things the Christian needs most are the power to believe and the power to suffer, and these two things can be taught to us by the enemy. Not until we are ready to sink beneath the pressure do we often learn the secret of triumph. The Lord lets the devil act as drill sergeant in His army, teaching His children the use of His spiritual weapons. You should, therefore, "consider it pure joy, my brothers, whenever you face trials of many kinds, because you know that the testing of your faith develops perseverance" (James 1:2–3).

This indeed is to be "more than conqueror"—learning lessons from the enemy that will fit us for his next assaults. Then we can meet them without fear of defeat. There are some things, though, that cannot be easily learned. Our spiritual senses seem to require the pressure of difficulty and suffering to awaken all their capacities and to constrain us to prove the full resources of heavenly grace. God's school of faith is always trial, and His school of love is provocation and wrong.

Instead of murmuring against our lot and wondering why we are permitted to be so tried, let us glorify God and put our adversary to shame. This will wring a blessing from Satan's hateful and hellish hostility, and we shall find after a while that the enemy will be glad to let us alone for his own sake, if not for ours.

The spoils are ours

To be "more than conqueror" means that we not

only receive the victory but the spoils of the victory as well. When Jehoshaphat's army won their great deliverance from the hordes of Moab and Ammon, it took them three days to gather all the spoils from their enemies' camps. When David captured the camp of Ziklag's destroyers, he won so vast a booty that he was able to send rich presents to the elders of Judah. When the lepers found their way to the deserted camp of the Syrians, they found such abundance that in a single hour the famine of Samaria was turned into a time of abundance.

So it is that our spiritual conflicts and conquests have their rich reward in the treasures recovered from the hand of the enemy. How many things there are, which Satan possesses, that we might and should enjoy! Think of the rich delight that fills the heart when we expel the giants of ill temper, irritation, haste, hatred, malice and envy. These have long ravaged and preyed upon all the sweetness of our life. What a luxuriant land we enter into when we overcome these foes! Delightfully, the spoils of peace and love and sweetness and heavenly joy enrich us in the things where once they reigned.

How rich are the spoils recovered from Satan when, through the name of Jesus, he is driven from the body. The suffering frame that had groaned and trembled under his oppression springs into health and freedom, yielding all its strength to the service of God with the joy of a victorious life. What a rich reward comes to the home that has been rescued from the dominancy of the devil! That place once full of turmoil because of a drunken husband, shameful lusting, vanity, empty frivolity, heartless worldliness, bitter strife, evil speaking or anger, now is become a happy Eden, with

Even after we have received Christ's indwelling, there are depths and heights in "all the fullness of God" in which we more perfectly enter, in proportion as we allow the Holy Spirit to fit us for the deeper and higher experience. This is often what our severest trials are meant for — to give our spirit a vigor and a capacity that will enable us to rise to a higher place in the fellowship.

Spiritual discipline

Finally, this strength is established and perfected by spiritual discipline. "And the God of all grace, who called you to his eternal glory in Christ, after you have suffered a little while, will himself restore you and make you strong, firm and steadfast" (1 Peter 5:10). Every new experience of Christ's grace must be confirmed by some new discipline in the school of trial. Even after we have come to know God as "the God of all grace," we must suffer awhile so that this knowledge and experience of His grace will become established, strengthened and settled.

And so, we are ever passing on "from strength to strength." We find, like the giant oak, that the wildest winds, instead of tearing us from our foundation, only plant us deeper and root us more securely in the Rock of Ages.

God's Measureless Measures

When they measure themselves by themselves and compare themselves with themselves, they are not wise (2 Corinthians 10:12).

CORRECT MEASUREMENT IS IMPORTANT. Half an inch off the draper's yardstick makes a significant difference when the goods are delivered. The division of a hairline in a carpenter's rule might destroy all the calculations of the architect in the construction of the building.

A little boy once told his mother that he was six feet tall. When she doubted the statement, he assured her that he had just measured himself. His calculations were right, but his ruler was not; it was only about six inches long. This is the sort of rule by which many Christians measure themselves.

Two ways of measuring

There are two ways we humans measure ourselves. The one is by comparing ourselves to ourselves. The other is by comparing ourselves with others. Both are equally unwise methods, because each comes short of the divine measure.

Many have tried to measure up to their ideals and aspirations, the outreach and loftiness of their humanity. They tell us that they have lived up to their light and to their conscience and are satisfied with their opinions. They are content with their lives, and they finish by saying that anyhow, it is no one's business but their own. These people are measuring themselves by themselves.

Another slant on this first method is those who measure themselves by a past experience — some memory of blessing, some lofty mount to which they rose in the distant past. To these individuals, this experience becomes the type and ideal of all their life. There are many people trying to hold onto their past experience or trying to get it back again. Instead, they should remember that God is "able to do immeasurably more than all we ask or imagine" (Ephesians 3:20).

There are just as many people using the second method of measuring. They congratulate themselves on being as good as their role models. The result of this is to be seen in the human traditions and stereotyped patterns of Christian living by which so many are molding their lives. From this kind of measuring, Paul turned to reach up to God's measure. Forgetting the things that were behind him, he pressed toward the mark for the prize of the high calling of God in Christ Jesus.

We find a number of God's standards and measures referred to in the Scriptures, and one simple phrase expresses these measures — "according to." Just two words — but upon them many of the promises build, leading us higher and higher to the perfect will of God. Let us consider some of these measures.

The will of God

This is at once the limitation and the inspiration of our faith and prayer. "If we ask anything according to his will, he hears us" (1 John 5:14). "The Spirit intercedes for the saints in accordance with God's will" (Romans 8:27). Beyond this, our desires and aspirations cannot go, for in the will of God lie all the probabilities of blessing that a human life can receive. God's chief desire is for us to see how much blessing His will can bring. There is no more expansive prayer within the reach of faith than the simple sentence, "Your will be done" (Matthew 6:10).

This will of God is for our highest possible good. We know it includes our salvation, because "God our Savior . . . wants all men to be saved" (1 Timothy 2:4). We know it includes our sanctification, for "It is God's will that you should be holy [Greek—sanctified]" (1 Thessalonians 4:3). We know it includes our deliverance from physical problems, for Jesus has said, "I am willing. Be clean!" (Matthew 8:3). We know it includes every needed blessing that the obedient can require, for the Scriptures promise, "The Lord bestows favor and honor; no good thing does he withhold from those whose walk is blameless" (Psalm 84:11). The apostle's prayer for his beloved friends was that they might "be able to test and approve what God's will is—his good, pleasing and perfect will" (Romans 12:2).

Are you measuring up to this divine rule? Are you meeting all your Father's will? Have you learned to "live a life worthy of the Lord" so that you will "please him in every way" (Colossians 1:10)? May you come under the blessing of His benediction so that He may "equip you with everything good for doing his will, and may he work in us what is pleasing to him, through Jesus Christ, to whom be glory for ever and ever. Amen" (Hebrews 13:21).

His Word

"I am the Lord's servant. May it be to me as you have said." Such was the sublime response of Mary to the angel's astonishing message: "The Holy Spirit will come upon you. So the holy one to be born will be called the Son of God" (Luke 1:35–38). Never was faith put to a harder test. Never was woman asked to stand in such a delicate place of peril and possibility, of humbling shame and glorious, everlasting honor.

Realizing all that this might cost her, she meekly, unhesitatingly, without one question, accepted the stupendous promise and responsibility. She rose up to meet the divine measure with her submission, "May it be to me as you have said." Like an echo from heaven came back the divine benediction: "Blessed is she who has believed that what the Lord has said to her will be accomplished" (verse 45).

Are we living up to this great measure? Obedience is walking not according to the course of this world or to the moods of our capricious hearts. It is not by the standards of men or by the example of others and not even according to the traditions of the church. It is walking according to God's Word. Are we truly Bible Christians, and are we determined to believe and obey every word within these inspired and heavenly pages? If so, we shall be found in the way everlasting, for "the grass withers and the flowers fall, but the word of our God stands forever" (Isaiah 40:8), and "the man who does the will of God lives forever" (1 John 2:17).

The riches of His grace

"In him we have redemption through his blood, the forgiveness of sins, in accordance with the riches of God's grace that he lavished on us with all wisdom and understanding" (Ephesians 1:7–8). Peter speaks of this in a similar way: "In his great mercy he has given us new birth into a living hope" (1 Peter 1:3). This is God's standard and measure of salvation. He works and saves according to the riches of His grace. He abounds toward us in all wisdom and prudence. That is, He adapts His mercy to every variety of guilt. In His prudence and foresight, He anticipates every future emergency. He sees Peter from the beginning to the end of his career and accepts him "for better or for worse." And when the hour of his shameful fall is near, He is able to say, "I have prayed for you" (Luke 22:32).

Have you entered into the fullness of this measure? Have you understood it in its all-sufficiency for a lost world? May our faith look up from lost humanity to the mighty love of God and the "riches of his grace." "As far as the east is from the west, so far has he removed our transgressions from us" (Psalm 103:12).

The riches of His glory

Can we form any concept of the riches of His glory? Moses asked to see that glory but was told it was too bright for human eyes. Only in the distance and from behind could he dare to look upon it. The disciples saw a glimpse of it on the Mount of Transfiguration, but they were afraid of its brightness, and their eyes were overcome with slumber under its spell.

"The heavens declare the glory of God; the skies

proclaim the work of his hands" (Psalm 19:1). Some idea of the riches of God's power and majesty may be gathered from the vastness of the universe with its stars and planets of untold numbers. Most of us have, at times, allowed our minds to dwell on the multitude of these discoveries and calculations. Can you conceive of the actual magnitude of heavenly bodies hundreds of times larger than our world? Consider that our sun outweighs the world many thousands of times. Look at the stars beyond stars,

> Where system into system runs
> And other planets circle other suns.

The hand of God holds all these orbs. His will commands all these forces. His wisdom positioned all these spheres, and His power continually directs them in their course. His sceptre sways this mighty empire. His creative word called every portion of it into being. His providence upholds it every moment. His taste and goodness have adorned it with beauty and loveliness and enriched it with happiness and blessing. There is not a creature among its inhabitants, from the highest archangel to the lowest insect, that does not owe its being to His power and goodness.

And yet, all this is but the hiding of His power (Habbakuk 3:4), for His omnipotence could call millions of such universes into being in a moment. And all this is just a scaffolding for the glory that He is preparing for the abode of His redeemed! The riches of His glory will not be complete until the new heavens and the new earth emerge from the flames of a dissolving world. Then in the glory of God, the New Jerusalem will descend from heaven, where the streets are gold and the gates are pearl and the foundations are made with precious gems. There the thrones are raised, the crowns are set, the mansions are completed. There the glorified saints are shining "like the brightness of the heavens, and those who lead many to righteousness, like the stars for ever and ever" (Daniel 12:3), and we ourselves are crowned with all "the riches of his glorious inheritance in the saints" (Ephesians 1:18).

Only then will we understand something of the meaning of such verses as these: "I pray that out of his glorious riches he may strengthen you with power through his Spirit in your inner being, so that Christ may dwell in your hearts through faith" (Ephesians 3:16). "Being strengthened with all power according to his glorious might so that you may have great endurance and patience, and joyfully giving thanks to the Father, who has qualified you to share in the inheritance of the saints in the kingdom of light" (Colossians 1:11–12). "My God will meet all your needs according to his glorious riches in Christ Jesus" (Philippians 4:19).

It is according to the riches of His glory that He is working out the new creation in our hearts and preparing the more glorious temple of the soul for His own eternal abode. It is according to the riches of His glory that He is willing to strengthen the heart for all patience and longsuffering. And it is according to the riches of His glory that He is able and ready to supply all our need. There is nothing too hard for such a God, nothing too rich and glorious for His wisdom, grace and love. He looks at the littleness of our faith and cries, "Do you not know? Have you not heard? The Lord is the everlasting God, the Creator of the ends of the earth. He will not grow tired or weary, and his understanding no one can fathom. He gives strength to the weary and increases the power of the weak" (Isaiah 40:28–29).

Let us lift up our eyes and behold the glory of our God. Let us begin to walk as sons and heirs and claim something of the riches of His glory.

The resurrection and ascension of Jesus Christ

> I pray also that the eyes of your heart may be enlightened in order that you may know the hope to which he has called you, the riches of his glorious inheritance in the saints, and his incomparably great power for us who believe. That power is like the working of his mighty strength, which he exerted in Christ when he raised him from the dead and seated him at his right hand in the heavenly realms, far above all rule and authority, power and dominion, and every title that can be given, not only in the present age but also in the one to come. And God placed all things under his feet and appointed him to be head over everything for the church, which is his body, the fullness of him who fills everything in every way. (Ephesians 1:18–23)

The resurrection and ascension of Jesus Christ have become for us the pledge and the pattern of all that our faith and hope can claim. The power that God has shown in raising Christ from the dead and setting Him at His own right hand is the same power that we may expect Him to exercise in us who believe. "The riches of his glorious inheritance in the saints" is the standard of what we may share in our spiritual experience now. God has performed for us the most stupen-

dous miracle of grace and power and nothing can ever
be too hard or too high for us to expect from "the
God of our Lord Jesus Christ, the glorious Father"
(Ephesians 1:17).

The picture is a definite as well as a glorious one.
Step by step we can ascend to its transcendent and
celestial heights with our ascending Lord. And then,
as we gaze on His lofty preeminence, we are permitted to sit down by His side and claim all the fullness of
His glory as our own. All His ascension power and
majesty are not for His personal exaltation, but that
He might become the Head over all things for His
body the church. He takes His high preeminence as
our Representative and recognizes us as already seated
with Him in the heavenly place. His resurrection
therefore involves ours; His triumph, ours; His ascension, ours; and His rights are shared with us.

Do we require in our behalf the exercise of an authority that transcends all other authority? We have
but to remember that He is sitting far above all princi-
palities. Do we require a force to be exercised for us
that overmatches the mightiest forces of nature or of
evil? He is sitting far above all power and might. Do
we ask something that even natural law would seem
to hinder? God has already overcome natural law by
raising Christ from the dead. Are we confronted with
imposing names and despised by human pride? We are
sitting side by side with One who is exalted above
every name that is named.

All the events of the great world are but movements
of Christ's mighty hand primarily designed for those
who immediately take part in them. But ultimately
they are for the good of His church and the building
up of His kingdom. Men and nations are but puppets

in the hands of our anointed King, and God uses them for His wise purposes even when they are fulfilling their own pleasure. After the resurrection of Christ, and in view of His enthronement, there is nothing we need fear to claim, according to this mighty measure, as part of the riches of our inheritance.

Christ Himself

In Romans 15:5 we read the words, "as you follow Christ Jesus," or as in the King James Version, "according to Christ Jesus." This is the highest of all standards—higher even than His resurrection, ascension and glory. As He is, so shall we be when He appears, but even "in this world we are like him" (1 John 4:17). We "are not of the world any more than [Jesus is] of the world" (John 17:14). "My command is this: Love each other as I have loved you" (John 15:12). "Just as the living Father sent me and I live because of the Father, so the one who feeds on me will live because of me" (John 6:57). "As you sent me into the world, I have sent them into the world" (John 17:18). "But we know that when he appears, we shall be like him, for we shall see him as he is" (1 John 3:2).

These are but some of the verses that speak of our identity with Jesus and the mystery of His life in us. Not only is He our example, but He is our life. Although we are but miniatures of Christ, God expects us to be receiving and reflecting Him in all His fullness. He expects us to be showing His life as our life, His love as our love, His riches as our riches. We represent Him. Among men we dwell not as citizens of earth but of heaven.

Is Christ our Pattern, our living Head, our Divine Standard and Measure? Are we determined to have nothing less and to be nothing less? Shall we cease to copy men and follow only Him?

I have often noticed would-be artists in an art gallery copying the paintings of the masters. Coming back weeks later, I found them still working on their copy. Their work was not complete, but day by day it became more like the original. If these artists had begun to copy the work of the masters from their own recollection or concept, their efforts would have soon become cheap and worthless.

So let us always keep our eye on the heavenly standard and be satisfied with nothing less than living "according to Christ Jesus." God holds Jesus before us and bids us follow not a hurried concept of Him or the copies we see in others but the Original. As we continually look to Him, our concept of Christ will be continually corrected, enlarged and vivified until it is transformed to our inmost being, not only as the Pattern but as the Life of our life.

A young man came on board a ship bound for the interior of Zaire. Finding a party of missionaries, he asked them to relay a message to another missionary far into the interior. "When I left the missionary two years ago," he told them, "I promised to be Christ's man. Tell him that I am Christ's man still." Simple as this concept is, it is the truest and highest that mortal thought can reach. It is God's own divine measure of Christian life to be a "Christ man," living, loving, trusting, serving, suffering, overcoming, "according to Christ Jesus."

According to the power that works in us

"Now to him who is able to do immeasurably more than all we ask or imagine, according to his power that is at work within us" (Ephesians 3:20). "To this end I labor, struggling with all his energy, which so powerfully works in me" (Colossians 1:29). "We eagerly await a Savior from there, the Lord Jesus Christ, who, by the power that enables him to bring everything under his control, will transform our lowly bodies so that they will be like his glorious body" (Philippians 3:21).

In these passages we have God's present working referred to in two directions: first, in the believer's heart and second, in the sphere of providence and government. The one must ever keep pace with the other. God does work in the forces around us, but we must also allow Him to work within us. Otherwise, all the might of His providence will be to no avail for us. "He is able to do immeasurably more than all we ask or imagine," but it must be done in us. It is "according to his power that is at work within us."

All the forces of the train engine are limited and measured by its source of power. It may be built to pull a heavy load, but its ability is according to the measure in which the power flows through it. In like manner, God is waiting to work in each of us. Indeed, He is already working up to the full measure of our yieldedness. We may have all that we are willing to have. The Holy Spirit is always ahead of us, pressing us on to more than we have yet fully received. We may be sure that according to the measure of His inward pressure, there will always be the external workings of God's mighty hand. Whenever we find the wheels of His sufficiency working within us, we can be sure the wheels of His providence are moving in unison externally.

Let us so yield to His power, that we are responsive

to its slightest touch—so responsive that, like the Aeolian harp, it will answer to the faintest breath of the Holy Spirit as He moves upon the chords of our inmost being.

According to our faith

"According to your faith will it be done to you" (Matthew 9:29) was Christ's law of healing and blessing in His earthly ministry. This was what He meant when He said, "With what measure you use, it will be measured to you—and even more" (Mark 4:24). All of these mighty measures that we have discussed are limited only by the measures—vessels—that we bring to be filled. God deals out His heavenly treasures to us in these glorious vessels. Each of us must bring our cup, and according to its measure, we will be filled. But even the measure of our faith may be a divine one—the little cup may become enlarged through the grace of Jesus, until from its bottom there flows a pipe into the great ocean of His provision. If that connection is kept open, we shall find that our cup is as large as the ocean, and it can never be drained to the bottom! We must remember that He has said to us, "Have faith in God" (Mark 11:22), which might be translated, "Have the faith of God," and surely that is an illimitable measure.

A group of early missionaries to the country of Sierra Leone found life difficult. A short time after their arrival, three of their number died of malaria. Soon afterward, one of the remaining missionaries wrote a letter back to his home. He said that on his way across the Atlantic, he had been led to see the truth of divine healing and had taken the Lord Jesus as his healer. But after the shock of his friends' death, his faith seemed to be totally paralyzed.

It was at this moment that he sought the Lord in prayer. To his surprise, there came upon him a peace so beyond himself that he rose not only comforted but established in God's confidence. He was so assured that the Lord was his healer and keeper that he had no fear—even of the failure of his faith. He was able to say with humble and holy confidence that, come what may, he would trust the Lord alone. He was assured that his life and faith would be upheld until his work was complete.

His cup had broken, and all the water had leaked out. But a divine hand fused the break and opened up a connection with the heavenly fountain. Immediately his cup was not only full, but it was full forever with all the fullness of God. His old faith had died, and out of its grave had come the faith of God. He had passed out of himself and into Christ, and now he was able to meet the immeasurable promises with a trust as measureless and divine.

So let us rise into the fullness of Jesus and sweetly

> Find His fullness round our incompleteness,
> Round our restlessness, His rest.

10

Spiritual Growth

But grow in the grace and knowledge of our Lord and Savior Jesus Christ (2 Peter 3:18).

A MOTHER ONCE FOUND HER little boy standing perfectly still by a tall sunflower in the garden, his feet buried in the soil. "What are you doing?" she asked. "I'm trying to grow as tall as this sunflower," he replied. "I want to be a big man when I grow up."

How truly has our Master said of all our struggles to grow taller, "Who of you by worrying can add a single cubit to his height?" (Matthew 6:27). All the little fellow's stretching did not increase his height. He learned from his mother that growth would come by eating hearty meals, drinking plenty of milk and exercising in wholesome and happy play. By doing this he would grow up to be a man in due time.

The same principle is true in our spiritual life. Fretting and straining will not hasten our spiritual growth. God has revealed the secret of growth, and it is not much different from the mother's counsel to her son. Let us look at some of the principles.

Sanctification is the beginning

The apostle who gave us our text also set forth the principles of spiritual growth in the opening chapter of his epistle. There is no single paragraph in Scripture that more profoundly unfolds the depths and heights of Christian life than the first 11 verses of Second Peter.

The fifth verse is an injunction to grow in grace, but the preceding verses give us the starting point for this growth—the experience of sanctification. The people to whom this epistle is addressed are recognized as recipients of "his very great and precious promises" so that through them they could "participate in the divine nature and escape the corruption in the world caused by evil desires" (verse 4).

These two facts constitute the whole of sanctification. It is that experience by which we become so united with Christ that we become partakers of His nature. The person of Christ, by the Holy Spirit, comes to dwell in our hearts, and by that indwelling, He becomes to us the substance and support of our spiritual life.

The converted soul is a human spirit born from above by the power of the Holy Spirit. The sanctified soul is a human spirit wholly yielded to and possessed and occupied by God's indwelling presence. Such a person is able to say, "I no longer live, but Christ lives in me" (Galatians 2:20). The effect of this is that we are able to "escape the corruption in the world caused by evil desires" (1 Peter 1:4). God's indwelling excludes the power of sin and evil desire.

The Greek tenses here leave no room for doubt about the question of time and the order of events. This deliverance from corruption precedes the command to grow—it is even the basis of that command. The first phrase in verse 5 shows this to be true: "For this very reason"—that is, because God has provided for our sanctification, imparted to us His nature and delivered us from the power of sin—for this reason, we are to grow.

It is evident that we do not grow *into* sanctification. Rather, we grow from sanctification into maturity. This corresponds with the description of the growth of Christ Himself in the Gospel of Luke. "And the child grew and became strong; he was filled with wisdom, and the grace of God was upon him" (Luke 2:40). No one could say that He grew into sanctification, because He was sanctified from the first. But He was a sanctified *child*, who grew into manhood. Still later when Jesus was an adolescent, it is added, "Jesus grew in wisdom and stature, and in favor with God and men" (verse 52).

This same Christ is formed in each of us—formed as an infant—and grows, as He did on earth, into maturity in our spiritual life. In the same way, we grow into a closer union with Him and gain a more habitual and intimate dependence upon Him for all our life and actions.

The relationship of growth and grace

The same beautiful passage in Second Peter brings out the relationship between growth and grace with fullness and precision. "His divine power has given us everything we need for life and godliness through our knowledge of him who called us by his own glory and goodness. Through these he has given us his very great and precious promises . . . " (verses 3–4). Here we are taught that God has provided all the resources necessary for a holy and mature Christian life. These resources are provided for us through the graces and virtues of our Lord Jesus Christ, which we are called to receive and share. He has called us, not for our glory and virtue, but for His. It is the same thought that the apostle expressed in his first epistle: "that you may declare the praises of him who called you out of darkness into his wonderful light" (2:9). Another translation (*NASB*) of this same passage reads, "that you may declare the excellencies of Him who has called you out of darkness into His marvelous light."

We are to display the excellencies of Jesus to the world—His glory and virtue. He clothes us with His character and in His garments, and we are to exhibit them to men and to angels. These provisions of grace are brought within our reach through all "his very great and precious promises," which we may claim and turn into heavenly currency for every needed blessing.

This is the concept of Christian life given in the first chapter of the Gospel of John in that wonderful little expression, "grace for grace" (*KJV*), or "one blessing after another" (*NIV*). In other words, every grace that we need to exercise already exists in Christ and may be transferred into our life from His.

Upon the mountain, Moses was called to see and study a model of the Tabernacle. A few weeks later, this design could be seen being constructed in the valley below. When completed, it would be a facsimile of the one shown to Moses on the mountain. God's explicit command was, "See to it that you make everything according to the pattern shown you on the mountain" (Hebrews 8:5).

Corresponding to this is the tabernacle God is building in our lives. It is just as heavenly a structure as the other, but it is far more important. It is meant to be the residence of God. This structure also has its model in the mount, and by faith we may see the model of our life. It is the pattern and plan of all the graces that we exemplify and the life that is to be built up, worked out and established. All the material for our spiritual building is provided and ready, and the design is fully worked out in the purpose of God and the provisions of His grace.

All then is ready for the construction, but we must take these resources and materials moment by moment, step by step and transfer them into our lives. We do not have to make the graces ourselves, but we must take them, wear them, live them, exhibit them. "From the fullness of his grace we have all received one blessing after another" (John 1:16) — His graces for our graces, His love for our love, His trust for our trust, His power for our strength.

Spiritual growth and our responsibility

While it is true that all the resources are divinely provided, this does not justify a spirit of passive negligence on our part. In fact, it summons us all the more to diligence and earnestness in pressing forward in our spiritual career. This is emphasized when, after enumerating the resources of God's grace with strong emphasis, the apostle Peter adds, "For this very reason, make every effort to add to your faith."

There is to be no languid leaning on God's grace, no dreamy fatalism based on His almighty purpose and power. Instead, there is to be a strenuous and unceasing energy on our part in meeting Him with the cooperation of faith, vigilance and obedience. The provisions of God's grace are made the basis of Peter's exhortation to give earnest attention to this matter. For this reason — and because God has so abundantly provided for us and is so mightily working in our lives and hearts and delivering us from the power of sin—for this reason, "add to your faith."

It is the same thought that Paul expressed in Philippians: "Work out your salvation with fear and trembling, for it is God who works in you to will and to act according to his good pleasure" (Philippians 2:12–13). This does not mean that we are to work for our salvation. We are represented as being already saved. But our salvation is in its infancy. It is an inward principle of life that must be developed in every part of our life. To this we are to "make every effort" (2 Peter 1:5), an effort that often reaches the extent of "fear and trembling." When this happens, there rises a holy and solemn sense of responsibility to make the most of our spiritual resources and opportunities, because "it is God who works in [us]."

It is as if the finger of solemn warning were raised, as if He were standing and looking into our eyes and saying, "God has come. The Almighty has taken this matter in hand. The Eternal Jehovah has undertaken the work; therefore, be careful what you do! Let there be no laxness, no negligence and no failure on your part to meet Him and afford Him the utmost opportunity to fulfill in you all the good pleasure of His will and the accomplishment of His grand purpose for your soul."

In connection with the parable of the ten minas, I once read an impressive comment: Every servant is given, at the beginning of his spiritual life, an equal measure of spiritual resource. The difference in our spiritual lives is not to be found in an unequal measure of God's grace and power. The difference is in the way people use what they are given. One mina was given to each servant. Several used these minas well—one even increased his tenfold. But one servant had made no effort to increase his measure. He had wrapped it up in a piece of cloth and kept it hidden. The difference between the two servants was in their diligence.

The one man determined to "make every effort" to add to his faith. The other simply tried to keep what he had. He did nothing to increase it. Are we "making every effort" to make the most of God's divine resources, of His "very great and precious promises," of "the divine nature" within us?

Harmony of the parts

The verse employed to describe our spiritual progress is an unusual one and one full of exquisite suggestiveness. It expresses the idea of harmony by using a musical figure. Paraphrased, the passage might read: "Add to your faith virtue, knowledge, temperance, just as in a perfect musical harmony, one note is added to another and one chord to another until the majestic Hallelujah Chorus swells to heaven without one discordant part or omitted measure."

In the old Greek festivals, it was customary for some prominent and gifted person to organize a chorus group or special musical entertainment. The one to whom this high trust was committed was called the *choregos*. From this expression comes our word *choir*. This person was a type of choirmaster, and his business was to combine the voices, the instruments and the musical compositions in such a manner as to produce the most complete harmony.

The Greek verb based on this word, *epichorego*, means then to combine things in harmony. It is far more than a dry figure of arithmetic: "adding" to our faith. This verb gives us a beautiful musical metaphor.

Perhaps the thought that lies back of this figure — the fact that God wishes our Christian growth to be like the development of a sublime oratorio — is already anticipated. It is to be a growth in which all the parts are so blended and the entire effect so harmonious that our life will be like a heavenly song.

It is easy to grow in one direction and be strong in one peculiarity. But only the grace of God and the power of the divine nature within can enable us to grow up to Him in all things, "attaining to the whole measure of the fullness of Christ" (Ephesians 4:13). It is one thing to have faith and courage, but it is another thing to have the two blended with temperance and love. It is one thing to have self-restraint, but quite another to have it combined with knowledge. To have brotherly kindness is one thing; to have love toward all men is another. It is one thing to have godliness, but it is still another thing to have it in perfect adjustment with love. It is harmony with all the parts that constitutes the perfection of the song and the completeness of the Christian life.

Perhaps God has educated you in each of the graces. Now, however, He is instructing you in the blending of those graces in perfect symmetry. Your love will be rendered mellow and pleasant, like a perfectly proportioned face — not so remarkable for any single feature, but unique in the whole expression of its countenance. Indeed, the most beautiful faces are like that.

The power of the whole is derived from the intermingling and the tempering of one grace with another. It is the combining of courage with faith that makes faith effective. The addition of self-restraint along with patience keeps it from becoming fanaticism and zeal without knowledge. It is in the quality of temperance and self-control combined with knowledge that the elements of discretion and wisdom are developed. But self-control and self-denial need patience to save them from being transitory outbursts and to give them permanence and stability.

Without godliness, these qualities would leave us on a low plane, but this intermingling lifts them to the heights of heaven and makes them a living sacrifice on the altar of His glory. Even godliness alone would leave us narrow and cold. God, then, requires of us an inner linking with our fellow Christians. The culture of these social qualities brings us into loving fellowship with one another and lifts us out of ourselves into brotherly kindness. Yet even that would not be complete if the circle were not widened far beyond the range of Christ's people. We must love the whole world, even as God loves it — the unworthy, the unattractive and even those who hate us and repel us.

Notice the shades of holy character that the New Testament expresses. What a multitude of words the Holy Spirit has given us for the various forms of love and patience. The list includes: love, charity, brotherly kindness, tenderness, meekness, longsuffering, patience, forbearance, unity, gentleness. They are like many shades of a color — all in the same class, yet no two exactly alike.

A famous sculptor was visited by a friend on two occasions, the second time only a few months after the first. The friend was surprised to find on his second visit that the sculptor's work appeared unchanged. "What have you been doing these two months?" asked the friend. "I've been touching up certain features, rounding it here and there and raising others," replied the sculptor. "But why?" asked the friend. "These are mere trifles!" "Yes," replied the artist, "but these make perfection, and perfection is no mere trifle." This is the way God often works with us, taking years to perfect one small area of our lives. This constitutes the difference between the image of Christ being revealed in us or the image of a marred, broken, imperfect man.

The relationship of growth to steadiness

It is not a matter of personal preference whether we will grow or not. It is a vital necessity that we do grow, because only in growing can we be kept from retrogressing. This the apostle hints of in our text: "Be on your guard so that you may not be carried away by the error of lawless men and fall from your secure position. But grow in the grace and knowledge of our Lord and Savior Jesus Christ."

Growth is the remedy for declension, and we must grow or go backward. The same truth is expounded in Second Peter 1:8–9: "If you possess these qualities in increasing measure, they will keep you from being ineffective and unproductive in your knowledge of our Lord Jesus Christ. But if anyone does not have them, he is nearsighted and blind and has forgotten that he has been cleansed from his past sins." That is the experience of conversion—it fades away and becomes a dim recollection unless we press on to deeper and higher things.

Have we not seen someone genuinely converted and used of God for the salvation of others and then find out that they refused to go on to higher experiences? Sometimes they have even sidestepped the doctrine and experience of sanctification as an affectation or a form of fanaticism. Sadly, the day came when their experience faded, and they were plunged into some dark trial. God used this, though, to compel them to see the need of something higher. It is not possible for us to safely remain in any stereotyped experience. Indeed, it is necessary for us to grow with acceleration and to make more rapid progress the longer we continue in the Christian life.

From the Greek we learn that the expression "in increasing measure" means to *multiply*. If these things are in us and *multiplying*, then they will make us to be neither barren or unfruitful in the knowledge of our Lord Jesus Christ.

Let us not fail also to notice the striking antithesis of the terms in verses 5 and 8, adding and multiplying. Adding nine to nine makes 18, but multiplying them makes 81, or nearly five times as much. Everything depends upon the size of the multiplier. In spiritual arithmetic, the multiplier is God—infinitely higher than the largest digits of human calculation. God takes the surrendered heart and unites Himself with it, and the result is extraordinary!

Let us meet God's expectation and provision and press on from grace to grace and from grace to glory.

The relationship of growth to rewards

The end of our growth will be an eternal reward: "And you will receive a rich welcome into the eternal kingdom of our Lord and Savior Jesus Christ" (2 Peter 1:11). Then no struggle will be regarded as too severe, no self-denial will be regretted, no toilsome victory will be remembered as too trying. Indeed, these things will constitute the exquisite joy and recompense of our eternal homecoming. What a glorious promise!

The Greek word used here to describe our entrance into the kingdom is the same one used in referring to the *adding* to our faith of all the heavenly graces. It is the beautiful metaphor of the *choregos*. It will be even more than "a rich welcome" given to us on our arrival. The idea is that a whole chorus of heavenly voices will sing us home. We shall enter like warriors returning in triumphal procession from a hard-won and glorious victory.

The choir that will meet us will be the same choir that we gathered around us in our earthly conflict. The graces, the virtues, the victories, the triumphs of patience and love that we won, and perhaps had forgotten about, will all be waiting up there like troops of angels. Then all will gather around us and fit into the chorus of joy that shall celebrate our homecoming.

God sometimes gives us here a little taste of that ecstatic joy. We remember some ministry of love long forgotten or some friend whom we led to Jesus or some word or deed testified of by one to whom we were made a blessing through an act of self-denial or faithfulness. Then we find that the little service rendered to that person had been traveling around the world and blessing hundreds along the way. We are melted into grateful wonder and adoring praise.

Yet these are but approximations of what it will be then, when all that we have been permitted to suffer and do for Jesus will be found waiting for us. There on the threshold of Glory, the saints will be ushered in for their great triumphal procession into the eternal kingdom of our Lord and Savior Jesus Christ. How we shall rejoice that we were once permitted to suffer and sacrifice for Jesus! Oh, how some will wish that once more they might have the opportunity of winning such a welcome and gaining such a great reward!

Nothing that we can gain for God can ever be lost. May the Master help us to "make every effort" to make the most of life and all its opportunities with these resources of grace. By doing this, we lay up for ourselves treasures on high that shall never fade away.

11

Enlarged Work

Enlarge the place of your tent (Isaiah 54:2).

Many years ago a humble Baptist preacher stood in an English pulpit and announced this text at the opening of what was perhaps the first missionary convention of modern times. He then proposed the following divisions as the themes of his message: (1) attempt great things for God; and (2) expect great things from God. From these two inspiring propositions, William Carey proceeded to preach a sermon that became the watchword of the greatest Christian movement since apostolic days.

That was the birth of modern missions. Soon the speaker himself was a missionary to Calcutta, and today an army of missionaries carries forth the gospel message to a lost world. The preacher had been one of those whom the Lord delights to use—one of the weak and discounted. A humble cobbler, he had supported himself by his meager trade. But while his hands were busy with shoes, his heart was reaching out to a lost world. His eyes were often on the maps that lined the walls of his workshop, and he was constantly calculating and planning the world's evangelization.

Deep in his heart, a great longing for the lost millions of mankind burned, and Carey's sermon was simply the outbreaking of the pent-up fires that long had smouldered within. It was the voice of God to his generation. And it is the voice of God to another generation—ours! He is pointing to a world where untold millions are still lost, and He is saying to us "Enlarge the place of your tent, stretch your tent curtains wide, do not hold back; lengthen your cords, strengthen your stakes. For you will spread out to the right and to the left; your descendants will dispossess nations and settle in their desolate cities."

Look at the rest of what Isaiah said about enlarging our tents:

> Do not be afraid; you will not suffer shame. Do not fear disgrace; you will not be humiliated. You will forget the shame of your youth and remember no more the reproach of your widowhood. For your Maker is your husband—the Lord Almighty is his name—the Holy One of Israel is your Redeemer; he is called the God of all the earth. (Isaiah 54:2–5)

From this passage, three thoughts are suggested: enlargement, consolidation, divine resources.

Enlargement

God's plan for His work involves taking the weak and immature person and developing him or her to maturity. Using this mature Christian, He then multiplies His work, and the process starts again in another person. The work He has done for us is but a sample of what He can do and wants to do for all the world. The blessing that has filled and thrilled our hearts may be multiplied as many times as there are cities in the world. It can be reproduced wherever there are hungry hearts to fill and messengers to tell of the grace and fullness of Jesus. That humble work, which has grown up out of a "handful of corn on the top of the mountains," can become a mighty forest on all the mountains. It can "flourish like Lebanon" or "thrive like the grass of the field" (Psalm 72:26).

God has been making samples, but He can multiply them by the millions. Will we let Him use us for their reproduction? That is how they are multiplied. They are not manufactured like machines in a factory. They grow as seeds grow—like the oak by the acorns it drops into the ground or like the single grain of wheat that sometimes sends up 20 stalks from a single seed, each stalk bearing half a hundred more seeds.

God has given us a gospel so full that it needs a world for its field. He is revealing a plan for the Christian church that is much more than an association of congenial friends who listen once a week to an intellectual discourse or to musical entertainment and carry on by proxy a mechanical Christian outreach.

Instead, God is building a church that can be the receptacle of every form of help and blessing that Jesus came to give to lost mankind. It is to be the birthplace and home of new Christians, the fountain of healing and cleansing, a shelter for the distressed, a school for the training of God's children, an armory where believers are equipped for doing battle in His name. Christ wants such a place in every center of population in this sin-sick world.

The figure of enlargement is that of a tent. Its curtains are to be stretched forth and its cords are to be lengthened. The curtains are the promises and provisions of the gospel, and they will stretch as wide as any of our needs. The cords suggest lines of prayer, faith, love and service. Our Lord instructs us to lengthen the cords of prayer. Let us ask more, but also let the strands of faith be as long and as strong. Let us believe more fully for a wider circle than we have dared to believe for before. Let the cords of love be lengthened and used to draw men and women to Christ. Let our efforts for His kingdom reach a wider circle. Let us make the world our parish. As the bride of the Lamb, let us realize that all that concerns our Lord must concern us, for "[our] Maker is [our] husband—the Lord Almighty is his name . . . he is called the God of all the earth."

God has committed to our trust the gospel in all its fullness. Let us never rest until it is fully known in every corner of this world.

One other thing remains, though. We must also lengthen the cords of our liberality. The Lord is asking for our wealth to spread His gospel. We to whom this gospel has been such a blessing are especially called to take it as our trust for Him and send it everywhere. There are many open doors, and workers are being prepared as never before. When I think of the opportunities of using money for God, I could almost envy the men who own successful businesses.

God is going to send large amounts into the treasuries of consecrated work. If we are true to this trust, we will be a part of this great effort.

Consolidation

It stands to reason that the wider our work, the stronger it must be at its center. As the cords are lengthened, the stakes must also be strengthened. What are these stakes?

God's Word is the first. The larger our task, the more important it is that we be true to the great standard of truth, the Bible, the gospel of Jesus Christ.

This is the day of new theologies and inexact views of evangelical truth. More than ever, God requires us to stand faithful to the cross of Christ, the doctrine of man's sin and ruin, the great atonement, the inspiration of the Holy Scriptures, the person and work of the Holy Spirit and the certainties of future retribution and reward. Thank God, we do not have to resort to the novelties of rationalism to attract the multitudes. Give them rather the Living Bread, the atoning blood, the old but ever new story of Jesus and His love.

Personal holiness is the next safeguard of the Lord's work. God cannot trust an unsanctified or unconsecrated person with much of His work. Like Jonah, many mar their most successful work by letting self intrude. The more God entrusts to us, the more we must remain at His feet. May all who bear the vessels of the Lord be clean.

Without the spirit of self-sacrifice, no work can be glorious. Luxury is killing churches today, and the only remedy for it is the red blood of sacrifice. We must be willing to endure hardness as good soldiers of Jesus Christ. We must be indifferent to popularity and human praise. We must be willing to live with great simplicity and rigid economy and be willing to be misunderstood and persecuted. We must be glad to be the companions of the lowly and despised, to face toil, hardship or even death and to count all things but loss for Christ and His kingdom.

Only this kind of person can possess the world for Christ, and only this kind of soldier can march to worldwide victory. The illustrious brigades of rank and luxury will fail in the day of battle and prove to be but splendid pageants and dress parades. May God give us the spirit of scriptural faith, personal consecration and true self-sacrifice. Only then can He give us the world for Christ!

The figure of the tent suggests the idea of constant vicissitudes and humility. There is no proud architectural structure, but a simple tent, always changing and often taken down and moved forward. This world is not our place of rest. It is no place for great cathedrals, splendid establishments or ecclesiastical states. It is a place for continual advance and ceaseless aggression.

I fear that splendid edifices have been the greatest curse of the church. As long as the early Christians met in humble upper rooms, they had the power of God and godliness. But when they began to imitate the splendor of the world and vie with the architecture of imperial palaces and heathen temples, the Holy Spirit took His flight, and the world and the devil became paramount.

The days of the Jewish tabernacle were better days than those of Solomon's temple. Let us never forget the tent spirit or lose the pilgrim attitude. "Enlarge the place of your tent." He does not say to build a temple. May the Lord help us to enlarge our tents but never to leave them!

Divine resources

"Your Maker is your husband—the Lord Almighty is his name—the Holy One of Israel is your Redeemer; he is called the God of all the earth." This is the secret. We have One backing us who has infinite resources, and He is not only our King and Friend,

He is our Husband. He has given us all His heart and all His glory, and He will give us all the world for our dowry and our inheritance. This is the secret of successful work: to know Christ in this blissful and intimate relationship and to receive our work, by virtue of our union with Him, as the fruit of our marriage with the King of kings. So may He reveal Himself to us. Then, as His Bride standing at the threshold of His home and inviting in His lost and wandering children, it shall be true of us, "The Spirit and the bride say, 'Come!'" (Revelation 22:17), and the world will come to Him!

"Who knows but that you have come to royal position for such a time as this?" (Esther 4:14). Like Esther, we have been called to a kingdom so that we might use our place of right and power to save the world. God help us to so win people back to Him, to so bear them as His children and ours, that He shall truly be called "The God of all the earth" (Isaiah 54:5).